CAST IRON SKILLET
ONE-PAN MEALS

CAST IRON SKILLET ONE-PAN MEALS

75
FAMILY-FRIENDLY
RECIPES FOR
EVERYDAY DINNERS

JACKIE FREEMAN

SASQUATCH BOOKS
SEATTLE

To my original "kitchen monkeys," Jack and Cole. Swinging from the rafters, shouting from the rooftops, and taste-testing recipes, you two are always keeping me on my toes, culinary-wise and otherwise.

CONTENTS

Introduction: *Not My Grandmother's Skillet*   1

CAST IRON HOW-TOS (AND HOW-NOTS)   4

MEATLESS MONDAY EVERY DAY OF THE WEEK: VEGGIE AND EGG RECIPES   17

Orecchiette with Butternut Squash, Leeks, and Sage   19
Cheater's Skillet Spanakopita   21
Pasta Frittata with Piquillo Peppers and Artichokes   24
Caramelized Onion and Tomato Pie   25
Pan-Seared Gnocchi with Spinach and White Beans   29
Kimchi Fried Rice with Enoki Mushrooms and Tofu   30
Pasta e Ceci (Italian Pasta and Chickpea Stew)   33
Orzo with Asparagus, Peas, and Parmesan   34
Cauliflower and Eggplant Masala   37
Thai Green Curry with Tofu and Rice Cakes   39
French Onion Soup-Strata   41
Pisto Manchego (Spanish Ratatouille)   42
Harissa Chickpeas with Eggs and Chard   44
Three-Bean Tamale Pie   45
Black Bean Chilaquiles with Eggs   49

A FISH OUT OF WATER: SEAFOOD RECIPES 51

Baked Cod with Artichokes, Sun-Dried Tomatoes, and Olives 52
Pan-Seared Salmon with Braised Lentil Salad 55
Brown Butter Halibut with Celeriac 56
Skillet Shrimp "Boil" with Potatoes, Corn, and Sausage 59
Clam Fideos 60
Thai Red Curry Rice with Halibut 63
Scallop Orzotto with Fennel, Orange, and Goat Cheese 64
Weeknight Orzo Paella with Mussels and Chorizo 67
Glazed Salmon with Black-Eyed Peas, Pomegranate Seeds, and Arugula 69
Skillet Mussel Marinara 73
Ginger Shrimp and Sugar Snap Peas with Coconut Rice 75
Clam and Bacon Pizza with Roasted Peppers, Kale, and Parmesan 79
Smoked Salmon Frittata with Cream Cheese, Capers, and Dill 81
Tuna Noodle Skillet Casserole with Peas and Prosciutto 82
Tomato-Poached Mahi Mahi with Zucchini and Fresh Herbs 85

TAKING FLIGHT: POULTRY RECIPES 87

Miso Chicken with Bok Choy and Mushrooms 89
Curry Poached Chicken and Couscous Salad 91
Turkey Pot Pie with a Twist 95
Edamame-Ginger Rice with Chicken 96
Roasted Chicken with New Potatoes, Coriander, and Mint 99
Turkey Skillet Chili with Cheddar Buttermilk Biscuits 101
Glazed Chicken Drumsticks with Warm Carrot Salad 103
Chicken Tagine with Spiced Fennel Quinoa 107
Easy Chicken Enchilada Skillet 109
Roasted Chicken with Braised White Beans and Bacon 110
Seared Duck Breasts with Fig and Arugula Salad 113
Orange-Tarragon Cornish Game Hens with Roasted Beets and Pistachios 114
Parmesan Chicken Tenders with Warm Fennel, Apple, and Arugula Salad 117
Chicken Thighs with Broccolini, Lemon, and Israeli Couscous 119
Dijon-Roasted Chicken with Italian Sausage and Brussels Sprouts 123

COWABUNGA: BEEF RECIPES   125

Stir-Fried Teriyaki Beef with Broccoli   127
Skillet Inside-Out Taco Bake   129
Meatballs with Caramelized Onions and Pine Nut Lemon Rice   130
Steak Tips and Cauliflower "Caponata" Salad   133
Cheeseburger Macaroni   135
Reuben Dutch Baby   136
Herb-Crusted Flank Steak with Sauteed Grapes and Blue Cheese   139
Skirt Steak Street Tacos with Corn and Black Bean Salad   141
Classic Patty Melts with Caramelized Onions and Cheddar   143
Pan-Seared New York Steak with Tarragon Mustard and Spring Vegetables   144
Beef, Green Bean, and Pineapple Red Curry   147
Good Ol' Beef Pot Pie   149
Root Vegetable and Beef Skillet Gratin   151
Spiced Beef and Chickpea–Stuffed Pitas "Kawarma"   155
Seared Rib-Eye Steak with Wilted Napa Cabbage   156

NOT QUITE KOSHER: PORK RECIPES   159

Pork Chops with Cashew-Lime Rice   161
"The Kids' Favorite" Skillet Lasagna   163
Grits-Crusted Ham and Cheese Quiche   164
Mustard-Coated Pork Tenderloin with Green Beans and Potatoes   167
Bacon and Poblano Grilled Cheese   168
Pork Ramen with Bamboo and Mushrooms   171
Chorizo and Sweet Potato Quesadillas   173
Caraway-Crusted Pork Tenderloin with Sauerkraut and Apples   177
Yam and Beet Hash with Italian Sausage   178
Super-Fancy Bacon and Porcini Skillet Nachos   181
Sesame Pork Cutlets with Warm Mustard Greens   183
Harissa Pork Chops with Eggplant, White Beans, and Tomatoes   185
Winter Squash Couscous with Pancetta   186
Skillet Maque Choux with Andouille Sausage   189
Roasted Bratwurst with Apples, Radicchio, and White Beans   190

Acknowledgments   193
Index   195

INTRODUCTION:

Not My Grandmother's Skillet

One pan to rule them all. One meal to feed them all.

Cast iron pans are often passed down from generation to generation. Fond memories of grandmothers frying chicken or making cakes in their perfectly seasoned skillets. Mothers simmering stews or roasting meats in the Dutch oven all day long. Their children and grandchildren inheriting precious family heirlooms and long-lived recipes as they receive these skillets when they move into homes of their own.

Well, my grandmother did own cast iron pans. And they were passed down to my mother. But honestly, I never saw either of them cook a single meal with those skillets once. I found our "heirlooms," rusted and dry in a box tucked into the corner of my parents' basement, simply by accident when looking for other kitchen utensils. The matriarchs in my family were not of the cooking persuasion, so their cast iron was abused and abandoned. But something about these skillets made them keep the pans around anyway. And I'm sure glad they did.

When I discovered these lonely, rusty cast iron skillets, I literally hugged them in my arms and jumped for joy (which is difficult to do . . . they are quite heavy). After much research, trial and error, and a few bad meals (but a lot of good ones to follow), I was able to revive those forgotten relics and start to make mealtime memories of my own. In the years that followed, I expanded my collection from a few forgotten skillets to a range of Dutch ovens, grill pans, and a few specialty cast iron items as well.

Perhaps like my grandmother and mother, you are wary of cooking with cast iron pans. Yes, they do require a bit of work (but doesn't anything that is worthwhile?), and they are heavy enough to squash even the most audacious arachnid. But with a little knowledge and practice, you may discover that your cast iron skillet becomes the most reached-for cookware in your kitchen. Naturally nonstick, an ace at achieving perfect sears on proteins and golden crusts on baked goods, these pans are versatile and durable. As we learn to make these one-pan meals together, I'll show you how to perfectly care for your cast iron so they last for generations to come.

The results of finding that hidden treasure trove of long-forgotten cast iron? This cookbook, which includes a range of recipes for every palate and skill level, from simple and easy to a bit more challenging (but never out of reach). Whether it's a normal weeknight (or morning) meal, a celebratory dinner with family and friends, or a cookout in the backyard, you'll find something to please every diner.

Though there are many cast iron books available on the market, few focus specifically on one-dish meals. I love sides, sauces, condiments, and baked goods as much as the next person, but this book is all about the center stage. It's time for breakfast, lunch, or dinner (or breakfast for dinner, if that's your thing), all in one skillet, all ready to go. Because we're busy, we're hungry, and we're ready to get out of the kitchen and do other things with our time.

It may not have the shine of copper or the sparkle of Teflon, but cast iron is here for the long run. It's affordable, it's versatile, and it's useful. And if you learn how to properly take care of it and use it, it will be a lifelong companion. Heck, you can even pass it down to your children and grandchildren. It's the everyday pan for the everyday cook for the everyday meal.

CAST IRON HOW-TOS (AND HOW-NOTS)

There are many tips and tricks to creating a perfect meal: choosing the perfect recipe and ingredients, seasoning properly, using the right cooking technique, and frankly, a bit of luck. There are also many tips and tricks to creating that perfect meal in a cast iron skillet. And, funnily enough, they are similar to the things you need to do to create that perfect meal. You'll need to choose the right recipe and ingredients, season the skillet properly, use the right cooking technique and tools, and again, a bit of luck. So, before you dive into the amazingly delicious and surprisingly easy one-pan meals in this book, take a few moments to learn more on how to get the most out of your cast iron skillet.

I know that you may not actually continue reading from this point. Tsk, tsk. But because I like you, and I know you're probably super hungry, and the doorbell is ringing, and the kids are whining, and the dog needs to go for a walk, and you just want to make dinner *now*, here is the abridged version so you don't get in too much of a muddle.

Cardinal rules for caring for cast iron:

1   Never, ever, ever, ever put your cast iron skillet in the dishwasher. If you do, I will find where you live, come to your house, and give you a very stern talking to. Why? You will spend days to decades building a perfect nonstick patina (coating) on your cast iron, and one rinse cycle later it will all be stripped off by harsh dishwashing detergents.

2   Never use soap on your cast iron. See the consequences of number 1, above. Yes, it may take off that beautiful seasoning. But, more importantly, you just really don't need to throw any soap on your skillet. The beauty of cast iron is that once it's perfectly seasoned, it's better than nonstick. A simple wipe with a soft brush or scrubber (and every once in a while, a firmer hand with a stronger brush or scrubber) is all it takes to get your skillet sparkly clean.

3   OK, this one may be more of a personal preference than an iron-clad rule: keep those metal utensils away from your pans. Reach for wooden or plastic instead. I also prefer to use a plastic scrubber (the cheap kind you get at the dollar store) versus a steel- or copper-wool scrubber for cleaning. However, it *is* OK to invest in a chain-mail scrubber for cleaning those occasional rough spots. It's like an itsy-bitsy suit of armor made just for your skillet. But just because the scrubber is

tough, that does not give you permission to go medieval on your cast iron. Scrub gently so you don't lose your patina.

4   Some folks say to never cook anything acidic (think tomatoes or vinegar) in a cast iron pan. Yes, the acid can damage the seasoning and impart a slight metallic flavor to your food over time, but the better seasoned your pan, the safer it will be. So go ahead and whip up that tomato sauce, just don't let it sit for hours.

5   Always let your skillet cool before tossing it in the sink. If it's too hot, your skillet could crack when hitting a pool of cold water.

6   Did your meal get over-aromatic? Using a plastic scrubber, scrub and rinse your pan under hot water until it's clean again. If you've cooked a dish that is especially fragrant (lots of onions, garlic, or curry, for example), scrub your pan with a mixture made from 1 tablespoon coarse sea salt and 1 tablespoon olive or vegetable oil to get rid of the funky smell, then wipe it clean.

7   Once your pan is clean, dry it on the stove top over low heat. When warmed through, rub your skillet with a bit of olive or vegetable oil and let it continue to warm for a few minutes more.

8   Let your skillet cool completely before storing.

9   When it comes to storage, you have two options: The best is to keep your cast iron front and center on your stove top or an open rack in the kitchen. This will allow it to "breathe" so that it doesn't accumulate any moisture that would cause it to rust. Also, you tend to use what you see, so if you see your skillet, you'll use it more. The other option, if stove-top space is at a premium, is to stack your cast iron in your (dry) cabinet with a layer of paper towels in between each pan to absorb any extra moisture in the air.

MORE THAN JUST AN AVERAGE-LOOKING PAN: HEALTH AND COST BENEFITS TO OWNING CAST IRON

Cooking in a cast iron pan, besides making food taste great, can actually make food a bit healthier and can be very budget friendly!

1   A well-seasoned skillet requires a lot less oil.

2   Cast iron releases a small amount of iron into your food, adding a touch of iron to your diet. Our bodies need a bit of iron to make hemoglobin (a protein found in red blood cells) to carry oxygen from our lungs to the rest of our bodies. Our bodies also require iron to produce some hormones. So, when you think about it, if we need iron to breathe, then cast iron is life, right?

3 Cast iron is almost indestructible, which means you only need to purchase one pan (or maybe a few, depending on how much you love cast iron . . . no judgment) for the rest of your life. And if you're lucky enough to inherit a cast iron skillet from a relative or rescue an abandoned skillet from a garage sale or thrift shop, they're practically free.

4 Best of all, cast iron is naturally nonstick, so you can avoid all of those pesky chemicals (like perfluorooctanoic acid) that are used to make nonstick pans. When treated nonstick pans (like Teflon) are heated to high temperatures, they release PFCs (perfluorinated compounds) into the air and your food. And when those pans are scratched, they release even more of those nasty chemicals into your food. These chemicals also make their way down the drain, polluting waterways, and find their way back into the food chain. It's a never-ending cycle of chemicals that take years to biodegrade. Hard pass; I'll just stick with naturally nonstick cast iron, thank you very much.

SIZE (AND SHAPE) MATTERS: HOW TO CHOOSE YOUR CAST IRON SKILLET

Cast iron skillets come in a variety of shapes and sizes to suit any meal. They are also available at a wide range of prices. If you aren't lucky enough to have these passed down from your parents or grandparents or find them at a garage sale or secondhand store, you can easily buy them online or at a local hardware or boutique store, for anywhere from $20 to $300. You can use them on the stove top (gas, electric, or induction), in the oven, on the grill, or over an open fire.

Skillets, also known as frying pans, have straight sides and long handles. They can range from 6 to 15 inches in diameter and are 1 to 2 inches deep. (Check out the bottom of your skillet for a size indication.) Larger skillets have loop handles on either side to make them easier to move around (because they are heavy!). Skillets are ideal for sautéing, searing, frying, broiling, and even baking.

Most often, you'll find skillets that are 8, 10, or 12 inches in diameter with a depth of 2 inches. Does it matter which size you use? Well, yes and no. Doing a bit of fancy and totally non-exact kitchen math, an 8-inch skillet holds about 7 cups (100 cubic inches), a 10-inch skillet holds about 10 cups (144 cubic inches), and a 12-inch skillet holds about 14 cups (202 cubic inches). That's quite a big difference, volume-wise. More forgiving recipes (think stir fries, sandwiches, pastas) won't mind the difference. However, your breads, cakes, and pizzas might be enraged. They either won't fit properly in the pan or will have vastly different baking times than the original recipe calls for. (A small side note: Don't even bother with a 6-inch or

14-inch skillet. The first is grossly too small to do much good, and the latter is so heavy you'll need a friend or family member to help you move it about the kitchen.)

For this book, we're keeping to the basics. Honestly, I used what I had on hand, and that was my grandmother's 10-inch cast iron skillet. All of these recipes were tested in a 10-inch skillet. For the most part, they will hold up in an 8-inch skillet (might be a little tight to fit everything in) or a 12-inch skillet (lots of wiggle room). But for the safest bet, stick to a 10-inch pan.

TOP IT OFF: Most skillets do not come with a lid. But most meals benefit from some time with the skillet covered. What to do? Invest in a 10-inch ovenproof lid with a heat-resistant handle so you can pop it in and out of the oven as needed. If you don't have a lid handy, a large piece of aluminum foil will usually get the job done.

PLEASE TAKE CARE: HOW TO SEASON (OR RESEASON) YOUR CAST IRON SKILLET

Yes, taking care of your skillet requires a little bit of work. But there's a reason that these bad boys have been around for centuries. They're tough, forgiving, and reliable (much like a beloved family pet or spouse). And if you take care of them, they'll take care of you. So don't fear the skillet and don't fear the care of the skillet. Once you practice a few times, you'll discover that it is easier to maintain than you think.

Most new skillets come ready to go: they are preseasoned at the factory so you can get cooking right away. However, the more you use your pan (and I hope that is a lot), the more you will lose that patina (the nonstick surface), so you will have to do maintenance. If you pick up a cast iron skillet from a friend, family member, or at a garage sale, how do you know if it's seasoned? If its color is gunmetal gray instead of a rich, shiny, black patina, it's time to season.

Every once in a while, your skillet might need reseasoning. You'll know it's time if food is sticking too much or it has been stored incorrectly and there is rust. Some folks even like to reseason at the beginning of every year just to make sure their cast iron is ready for the work ahead. If any of this is the case, simply follow the initial steps on page 10 to season your skillet, but skip the soap used to wash it.

Proper seasoning and care of your skillet bakes the oil into the porous surface to create that perfect nonstick surface and helps prevent your pans from rusting (they are made of iron, after all). If you need to season your skillet for the first time (or reseason it after years of abuse or neglect), follow these steps:

1 Preheat the oven to 400 degrees F.

2 Wash your pans with warm soapy water and scrub with a stiff brush or steel wool. Rinse with warm water and dry completely (with a kitchen towel, paper towel, or by drying over low heat on your stove top). Make note: This is the *only* time you will use soap on your cast iron. For the love of all that is holy, never use soap for regular cleaning between cooking. (Check out my cardinal rules for regular care of your cast iron on page 4.)

3 Using a paper towel, rub the pan, on the inside *and* the outside (don't forget the handle too), with a thin coating of olive or vegetable oil (this will melt right into

CAST IRON COOKING METHODS

You might already know this, but there's nothing your cast iron skillet can't do. Here's a rundown of different cooking techniques you will be putting to use with these recipes:

BAKING: Most of us don't equate cast iron skillets with delicious baked goods, but hear me out. That even, hot heat helps form golden and crisp crusts while maintaining a delicate and moist interior to our cakes, breads, pies, and other baked goods, sweet or savory.

BRAISING: If you want to turn tough cuts of meat into tender morsels, you want to braise. The key is to first sear your meat in a bit of fat so it develops a golden-brown crust (this works for ground beef too, otherwise you end up with that flabby gray spongelike mess). Once your meat is caramelized, deglaze with a bit of booze (wine, beer, spirits, or even chicken stock or apple juice), add your main liquid, and simmer away.

FRYING: There is a reason your grandmother made fried chicken in her cast iron skillet and not any other skillet, and why that pan had an amazing dark patina and the best qualities of a nonstick pan ever made. All of that oil soaked into the porous surface of the pan, after years of cooking, creating the perfect pan for your food. Now we may not want to deep-fry our food every day, but a deep-fried chicken thigh or donut every now and then is a worthy treat and a great use of your skillet.

GRILLING: When you don't have the time, appropriate weather, or patience to fire up the grill, turn to your cast iron cookware. You can achieve a nice, rich, almost smoky flavor with the deep, sustained heat of cast iron. If you really want to achieve a certain look, you can buy cast iron skillet grills. Don't forget, if you do want to fire up the grill, your cast iron works great outdoors (heck, that was its original use!).

all of those pores). You'll know you have enough oil if you basically can't see any once it's rubbed in.

4   Place the pan upside down on a baking sheet lined with aluminum foil (to catch any drips), and bake for 1 hour. Let it cool in the oven. Depending on how much abuse your pan has suffered, you may need to repeat this process a few times until you reach that perfect patina (a rich, dark, and shiny black surface).

5   Store your cast iron with a paper towel used as a liner to keep it clean, dry, and to help absorb any excess oil or moisture.

PAN-SEARING: Again, it's all about the crust. Searing protein (whether it's beef, pork, chicken, fish, or even a slab of tofu) locks in flavor and moisture. Season your protein with salt, pepper, or spices while you preheat your cast iron. Add a bit of fat in the form of oil or butter, then sear both sides. If the protein sticks to the pan, don't try to wiggle it free—that means you need to cook it for a few moments or minutes longer to allow it to naturally release.

ROASTING: This is similar to braising, except it uses a dry method of cooking. It's like having your very own hearth oven. Add a bit of oil or ghee (regular butter has a tendency to burn at high heat) to your preheated pan, then toss in your veggies or protein. Add the skillet to a hot oven and let it roast away.

SAUTÉING: This is a cousin to the pan-sear. Cook foods in a bit of fat and toss around until they are just tender and golden. It's quick, it's easy, it's dinner!

STIR-FRYING: No, you don't need a wok to stir-fry. Yes, you can use a cast iron skillet. Choose a skillet with deep sides so you can toss ingredients with (almost) reckless abandon. Cast iron is ideal for this type of cooking, as you can get the pan superhot and need only a tablespoon or so of oil to cook the food quickly. Before you start, make sure that all your food is prepped and ready to go, because once you start cooking, things move quickly. Choose high-heat oils (think peanut, sesame, or vegetable) so your pan (and food) doesn't start to smoke (in an unpleasant way). Cook your food in batches (veggies, then protein, then sauce) so the items fry instead of steam.

NOT REALLY COOKING, COOKING: Remember how we talked about that long, even heat that cast iron is famous for? Well, that heat sticks around for a long time after the pan has been removed from the cooktop, oven, or fire. Use that residual heat for a second, lighter cook. You can toast bread (garlic or plain) or make a quick pan sauce or gravy.

STICKY BUSINESS: If, after seasoning, your pan is sticky, it usually means either (1) you used too much oil, (2) there was not enough heat (check your oven temperature to make sure it's accurate), or (3) you didn't bake it long enough. If you cheated a bit on any (or all) of these, give your cast iron a good scrub to remove the sticky layer and try again.

A NOTE: Seasoning (or reseasoning, as the case may be) from scratch is a little stinky. The oil on your pans will start to smoke a bit. This is not good for cooking, but OK for the seasoning process. Make sure you have a fan running or a window open while your cast iron bakes.

WHEN THINGS ARE REALLY, REALLY, REALLY BAD: Despite our best intentions, sometimes skillets get so abused that they need a complete restoration. Whether they are covered in rust, grime, or grease, there are a couple of methods to bring your skillet back to life.

1   Elbow grease: Usually the best method to get rid of rust and grime is brute force. Remove any loose pieces of food with a nonmetallic scraper, then scour the skillet with steel wool or a brass scrubber and a combination of equal parts coarse sea salt and olive or vegetable oil. Scrape, scrub, then season per the directions on pages 10 and 11.

NOT JUST FOR COOKING: WHAT ELSE CAN MY CAST IRON DO?

Besides cooking delicious food, your cast iron skillet can also . . .

WORK AS A PANINI PRESS. Place your sandwich to be pressed in a larger skillet, then stack a smaller skillet on top. Check out some great sandwich recipe ideas in *A Hearty Book of Veggie Sandwiches: Vegan and Vegetarian Paninis, Wraps, Rolls, and More.* Authored by yours truly, of course.

MELLOW THE HEAT. If you're always burning butter, pasta, mashed potatoes, or other food in the bottom of your "regular" pans while trying to keep them warm on the stove top, place them on top of your cast iron skillet as a little diffuser.

THAW MEAT QUICKLY. If you have a thin frozen steak, fish fillet, or pork chop that you forgot to defrost in the fridge overnight, you can place it on top of a cast iron skillet (without heat) at room temperature. Let it sit for about an hour, and the skillet will help to transfer ambient heat from the metal to the food. Make sure to wash and oil your skillet afterward to avoid any cross contamination.

2   Into the fire: If you have a seriously damaged or rusted pan, you can totally strip
    the skillet by running it through the oven's self-cleaning cycle or throwing it in
    a campfire and removing it once the fire extinguishes.

TURN UP THE HEAT: HOW TO COOK WITH YOUR CAST IRON SKILLET

There is a misconception that cast iron heats evenly. I hate to be the one to break
it to you, but . . . it actually doesn't heat evenly, because of its thermal conductivity
(the ability to transfer heat from one part of the metal to another). However, what
it does do is hold on to the heat evenly. Once your pan is hot, it will stay hot in a
more even manner than other pans you may have in your kitchen (looking at you,
stainless steel and aluminum). This is great for searing room-temperature steaks
in a hot pan (because the temperature of the pan won't drop) or getting a perfect
golden crust on your next baked good. Teflon-coated and stainless-steel pans tend
to "sweat" your food, which ends up stewing (and toughening) your meat instead
of browning it, and can ruin a golden-brown crust in a heartbeat. Cast iron skillets
provide sustained dry heat because the porous surface prevents excess moisture
in the pan, resulting in even browning and killer crusts. The even exchange of
heat also allows your food to brown and caramelize better than it would in those
other pans. Remember, though, because of cast iron's superb heat retention, if
you're trying out a recipe you'd usually make with a different cooking vessel, it will
continue to cook once pulled from the oven or stove top (for example, chocolate cake
may need a slightly lower temperature or less baking time).

One of the other advantages of using cast iron is that it can go anywhere. Start
cooking on the stove top, then transfer your dish to the oven or broiler to finish.
No problem! If you're working with ingredients that cook at different rates (think
carrots versus scallops), you can start one earlier and let it cook a bit longer (carrots,
then scallops) or sear your protein and keep it warm while cooking the remainder of
the meal (scallops, then carrots).

Cooking with gas or electricity? Some worry that you can't use a cast iron skillet
over electric heat. Never fear. It may take a bit longer to heat and cook your food, but
electricity works perfectly well. Simply add a few minutes to the process, paying
close attention to how your food is reacting. If you have a glass-top cooking range,
remember that cast iron pans are very heavy, so carefully move them and gently
set them down. Never slide them across a glass surface (insert nails-on-chalkboard
sound here).

The basics when it comes to cooking:

- Because cast iron maintains such an even heat so well, you rarely need your stove-top temperature above medium. Heat the pan all the way through before cooking, otherwise your food just sort of sits there and sticks. How do you know if your skillet is hot? Drop a few sprinkles of water in the pan—when your skillet is ready, they'll dance around and then evaporate.
- Those handles get wicked hot. So always make sure to have an oven mitt, insulated or silicone handle cover, or a dry kitchen towel on hand to grab the handle. And the pans stay hot for a long time after being removed from the heat, so place them on a trivet, not your Formica countertops. As a general safety rule, since I have kids and a husband around, I always leave an oven mitt on the handle until the pan is completely cool, as a bit of a heads-up to those in the kitchen who may indiscriminately grab at the handle to move the pan.
- Those skillets can be super heavy! It's always "arm day" at the gym when cooking with a cast iron pan, so use two hands for an even workout.
- Cast iron does not make for a good storage or travel container. The iron can impart a slight metallic taste if the food sits for too long. Eat your dinner and pack up the leftovers in another storage container.

ONCE THE JOB IS DONE: HOW TO TAKE CARE OF YOUR CAST IRON SKILLET AFTER YOUR MEAL

To keep your cast iron at its peak performance day after day, establish a little ritual. A few moments taken after every meal will save you hours of reseasoning in the long run. Practice this regular care every time you cook, no excuses.

1   After you've dined on your delicious creation, wipe the pan out with a paper towel to remove any bits and pieces of food or oil.
2   Let your pan cool a bit (so it's easier to handle) and rinse it under hot water. Scrub any stubborn areas with a nonabrasive scrub pad or work it a little bit with a chain-mail scrubber if there are some super-sticky spots.
3   Don't put your pan on a rack to drip-dry! Instead, place it back on the burner, over low heat, to get rid of any rust-causing moisture.
4   While you're there, using a piece of paper towel, rub a tiny bit of vegetable oil into the warm skillet, replacing the paper towel as needed, until the skillet looks shiny (but not greasy).
5   Let your skillet cool completely before you store it. If you're a die-hard cast iron cooking aficionado, simply place your skillet on the back burner so it's

immediately ready for your next meal (and stays nice and dry). If you like to cook with your cast iron just on occasion, store it in a dry cupboard, lined with a clean paper towel to absorb any moisture and excess oil and to keep it clean.

Sometimes your pans need a quick reseason—kind of like a spa day—when they get a bit dry, sticky, or dull. Just like you might treat yourself to a little refresher, don't shy away from giving your cast iron some love. How do you know it's seasoned? The surface of your pan should have a smooth, dark, glossy finish to it. It should not feel sticky (or, conversely, greasy). The easiest (and cheapest) way to test your pan is to fry an egg. If it slides out of the pan, you're good to go. If it sticks to the bottom, go ahead and give your pan a touch-up reseason.

1   Heat your pan over medium heat on the stove top. Give everything a good rub down with oil using a paper towel (see, just like a spa day!), wiping away any excess. Repeat this three or four times, applying oil and wiping away the excess, allowing the oil to soak into the pan's pores. Remove it from the heat and let it cool completely before storing.

2   If you find your pan is still a bit sticky, it's probably from food and oil buildup from use (way to go!). To clean your sticky skillet, simply preheat your oven to 400 degrees F, place the pan upside down on an aluminum-foil-lined baking sheet, and bake for 1 hour. Wipe it dry and let it cool before storing it properly.

TIP: Stinky pan? No problem. If your last round of fried fish or extra-garlicky sauce left your pan a bit aromatic, simply pop it in the oven at 400 degrees F for 10 minutes to get rid of any undesirable odors. Or give it a good old-fashioned scrub (see step 2 on page 14).

MEATLESS MONDAY EVERY DAY OF THE WEEK:
Veggie and Egg Recipes

Despite what some of my family members may think, not every meal, whether it be breakfast, lunch, or dinner, needs to be carnivorous. Yes, a nice steak, pork chop, or fillet of fish is wonderful cooked up in a cast iron skillet (just look at the recipes in the following chapters, because they are amazing), but life should be about balance. Leaving out the animal protein a few times a week is good for you (health-wise), your wallet (price-wise), and the environment (resource-wise). And for those who may be feeding the meat-and-potato-loving-or-I'm-leaving family member or friend, don't worry. Vegetarian mains still pack plenty of protein in the form of eggs, cheese, soy, and beans and leave you walking away from the table feeling full and happy. Heck, sometimes folks don't even realize they're eating a meat-free dish.

In this chapter, you'll find vegetarian meals that are hearty, filling, fun to make, good to look at, and absolutely palate pleasing, without the hoof, beak, or fin. There are even a few vegan mains (and a lot of dishes that can easily be turned vegan with some clever substitutes like dairy-free cheese, or tofu instead of eggs) if you're looking to try something new or eliminate something old. Some of these dishes are great for breakfast, some are great for lunch, some are great for dinner. Honestly, most are good for any meal throughout the day, so whip up these veggie and egg one-pan meals with reckless abandon!*

OK, OK. Let's not be too reckless with our cast iron. They are great tools that deserve our care and respect. Am I right?

ORECCHIETTE

with Butternut Squash, Leeks, and Sage

I think at some point we all learn the life lesson that looks can be deceiving. This dish is one of those lessons. At first glance, you would think this is nothing more than macaroni and cheese. But your first bite immediately lets you know that this is so much more. The pasta and sauce take on a luxurious flavor from slowly simmering in a bit of cream and butternut squash. The squash breaks down as it cooks, becoming silky, smooth, and rich, with just a touch of sweetness that is perfectly balanced by savory fresh sage. And yeah, OK, I put some cheese on top for good measure. I'm not a monster.

For time and convenience, I use frozen butternut squash (the kind that is already cubed). If you happen to have a fresh butternut on hand (or Hubbard, acorn, or sugar-pie pumpkin), peel and cube a little over 1 pound. Roast it until tender at 425 degrees F for about 30 minutes, tossing and checking every 10 minutes or so, and use that in lieu of the frozen stuff.

MAKES 4 TO 6 SERVINGS

½ cup (4 ounces) whole-milk ricotta cheese

½ cup (1½ ounces) shredded Parmesan cheese

1 teaspoon fresh lemon zest

Kosher salt and freshly ground black pepper

1 tablespoon high-heat oil, such as canola or safflower

1 medium leek (about 1 pound), white and light-green parts only, halved lengthwise, cleaned, and thinly sliced

2 (10-ounce) bags frozen butternut squash, thawed and drained

3 medium cloves garlic, minced

2 tablespoons chopped fresh sage

¼ cup dry white wine

6 ounces (about 2 cups dry) orecchiette pasta

1½ cups milk, water, or vegetable broth, plus more as needed

1 cup half-and-half

1 Combine the ricotta, Parmesan, and lemon zest in a bowl. Season to taste with salt and pepper. Set aside.

2 Heat the oil over medium heat in a 10-inch skillet. Add the leeks and cook until softened and just starting to brown, about 5 minutes. Stir in the squash, garlic, and sage and cook until fragrant, about 1 minute. Season to taste with salt and pepper. Add the wine and cook until almost completely evaporated, about 1 minute.

3 Add the pasta to the skillet, then carefully stir in the milk and half-and-half. Bring to a simmer and stir gently and often, uncovered, until the pasta is tender and the liquid has thickened, about 15 minutes. Add a touch more milk during cooking if needed. Season to taste with additional salt and pepper.

4 Preheat the broiler to high with the rack positioned in the top half of the oven.

5 Dollop the ricotta mixture evenly over the top of the pasta. Transfer the skillet to the oven and broil until the cheese is melted and just starting to have golden spots, about 4 minutes. Carefully remove from the oven and let cool for 10 minutes before serving.

CHEATER'S SKILLET SPANAKOPITA

The magic of spanakopita is the rich, creamy, and tangy spinach-and-cheese mixture wrapped in a multitude of perfectly flaky and tender sheets of phyllo dough. However, all of that magic takes a lot of work. This "cheater" version gives you the same great flavor and texture but is a kazillion* times quicker and easier. You get the fabulous filling with fresh pops of dill, mint, and lemon juice. And you still get that ethereal wrapping of phyllo present with every single bite. But instead of spending (what can feel like) hours painstakingly separating, buttering, then restacking moth-wing-thick phyllo sheets, in this version you simply spray the store-bought sheets with a bit of oil, crumple them into a ball, then plop them right on top of the filling. It's so easy, even a kid can do it.**

*An estimated quantity.
**Actual kids in my household have done it.

MAKES 6 TO 8 SERVINGS

2 tablespoons unsalted butter
1 medium leek (about 1 pound), white and light-green parts only, halved lengthwise, cleaned, and thinly sliced
1 pound baby spinach
4 medium cloves garlic, minced
Kosher salt and freshly ground black pepper
2 cups (about 8 ounces) crumbled feta cheese
½ cup (about 1½ ounces) shredded Parmesan cheese

2 large eggs, lightly beaten
¼ cup roughly chopped fresh dill
¼ cup roughly chopped fresh mint leaves
1 tablespoon freshly squeezed lemon juice
2 teaspoons fresh lemon zest
⅛ teaspoon freshly grated nutmeg
Pinch of red pepper flakes
20 (14-by-9-inch) frozen phyllo sheets, thawed
Nonstick cooking spray

1 Preheat the oven to 375 degrees F.

2 Melt the butter in a 10-inch skillet over medium-low heat. Add the leeks and cook until tender, about 5 minutes. Add the spinach in large handfuls and cook until wilted, 10 to 15 minutes. Stir in the garlic and season to taste with salt and pepper; cook for 30 seconds. Transfer the mixture to a bowl and set aside until cool enough to handle. Remove as much extra moisture from the spinach as possible, either by squeezing in your hands or placing the mixture in a clean dish towel and wringing. Discard the extra liquid and return the spinach to the bowl.

→

3 Stir the feta, Parmesan, eggs, dill, mint, lemon juice, lemon zest, nutmeg, and red pepper flakes into the spinach. Season to taste with salt and pepper. Spread the mixture evenly into the empty skillet.

4 Working with one sheet of phyllo at a time, lay it flat on a clean counter and spray it with the oil. Crumple the phyllo into a 2-inch ball and place it on top of the spinach mixture. Repeat with the remaining phyllo.

5 Bake until the phyllo is golden brown and crisp, about 25 minutes, rotating the skillet halfway through baking. Cool for 10 minutes before serving.

TIP: If fresh spinach is not available, you can swap it out with a 10-ounce bag of frozen spinach. Thaw it before use and make sure to squeeze every last drop of moisture out of it (I like to wring it in a clean kitchen towel). Cook it along with the garlic, increasing the cook time to about 1 minute.

PASTA FRITTATA

with Piquillo Peppers and Artichokes

Is it a pasta dish? Yes. Is it an egg dish? Also yes. This perhaps slightly unusual combination of pasta and eggs features a heavy sprinkling of Manchego cheese, bright notes and colors of (not-spicy) piquillo peppers, acidic artichoke hearts, and lemon zest. It is equally at home at brunch as it is at the lunch and dinner table. It's an unlikely hodgepodge that somehow works all together. And it's almost entirely made from common pantry and refrigerator ingredients. For the best flavor and texture, let some of that pasta stick out of the eggs so it gets crispy-crunchy when baking in the oven.

MAKES 4 TO 6 SERVINGS

6 large eggs

2 cups (about 6 ounces) shredded Manchego cheese

3 tablespoons extra-virgin olive oil, divided

3 tablespoons chopped fresh Italian parsley

1 tablespoon fresh lemon zest

Kosher salt and freshly ground black pepper

3 cups vegetable broth or water

6 ounces angel hair pasta, broken in half

1 (14-ounce) can quartered artichoke hearts, drained

½ cup jarred piquillo peppers, drained and chopped

1 Preheat the oven to 375 degrees F.

2 In a medium bowl, whisk together the eggs, cheese, 1 tablespoon of the oil, parsley, and lemon zest until well blended. Season to taste with salt and pepper.

3 Bring the broth and a large pinch of salt to a boil in a 10-inch skillet. Add the pasta and cook, stirring occasionally, until the pasta is tender and the liquid has evaporated, 7 to 10 minutes. Reduce the heat to medium, add the remaining 2 tablespoons oil, and continue to cook the pasta, scraping under the edge of the pasta with a wooden spoon until it starts to crisp, an additional 5 to 7 minutes.

4 Using the wooden spoon, push some of the pasta up the sides of the skillet so the entire skillet is covered with pasta. Carefully pour the egg mixture over the pasta. Gently push the pasta with the wooden spoon to allow the egg mixture to flow toward the bottom of the skillet. Sprinkle with the artichoke hearts and peppers.

5 Transfer the skillet to the oven and bake until golden brown and slightly puffed, about 15 minutes. Cool for 5 minutes before serving.

CARAMELIZED ONION AND TOMATO PIE

This pie is a labor of love but totally worth it. Take the time to deeply caramelize, and use the best tomatoes you can find: Summertime heirlooms will really sparkle with the creamy Parmesan filling. Dreary winter hothouse tomatoes will be a bit ho-hum (but still worth it if that's all you have). To make life easier, buy a prepared pie crust (refrigerated or frozen). Or you can certainly prepare your own crust for the best flavor. And this one is a bubbler in the oven, so you may want to place your skillet on a baking sheet before putting the whole kit and kaboodle in the oven. If you can't eat the whole pie at once, the leftovers are even tastier the next day. Or freeze slices, wrapped tightly in plastic wrap, for up to 3 months, then reheat them at 350 degrees F for about 20 minutes.

MAKES 6 SERVINGS

2 tablespoons unsalted butter
2 large yellow onions, thinly sliced
2 medium cloves garlic, minced
1 tablespoon chopped fresh thyme, or 1 teaspoon dried
Kosher salt and freshly ground black pepper
2 cups (about 6 ounces) shredded Parmesan cheese

½ cup mayonnaise
1 large egg, beaten
1 prepared pie dough
2 tablespoons dried bread crumbs, divided
2 pounds fresh tomatoes, cut into ¼-inch-thick slices

1 Heat the butter over medium-low heat in a 10-inch skillet. Add the onions and cook, stirring often, until deeply caramelized (a rich, dark brown), 25 to 35 minutes. Stir in the garlic and thyme and cook for 1 minute. Season to taste with salt and pepper. Transfer the onion mixture to a large bowl to cool slightly. Then fold the cheese, mayonnaise, and egg into the onion mixture.

2 Preheat the oven to 425 degrees F.

→

3   Roll the pie crust out into a 14-inch circle. Transfer the crust to your skillet, pressing it into the bottom and sides of the pan. Fold the edges under and crimp.

4   Spread one-third of the onion mixture onto the crust. Sprinkle with 1 tablespoon of the bread crumbs. Arrange half the tomatoes, overlapping slightly, on top of the bread crumbs. Repeat with another one-third of the onion mixture, the remaining 1 tablespoon bread crumbs, and the remaining tomato slices. Top with the remaining onion mixture.

5   Loosely cover the skillet with aluminum foil and bake in the oven for 15 minutes. Reduce the temperature to 375 degrees F. Continue to bake until the filling is tender, about 30 minutes more. Remove the foil and bake until the bread crumbs are golden brown, 5 to 10 additional minutes. Cool for 30 minutes before serving.

TIP: You can prepare the caramelized onions a day or two beforehand, then warm them up in the skillet when you're ready to prepare the rest of the pie.

PAN-SEARED GNOCCHI
with Spinach and White Beans

Plump gnocchi are gently cooked with spinach, white beans, and aromatics for an easy (yet somehow quite impressive) weeknight dinner. The trick to this dish is to cook it in stages. Start with the hardest ingredients (shallots and gnocchi), then work your way to the softest (spinach and beans) so that nothing overcooks. So think about layers, use a light hand, and then bask in the glow of your simply sophisticated meal. And as much as we all love fresh gnocchi, save it for another dish. You want to use the packaged stuff so you'll end up with the perfect texture in the final dish—a creamy pillow of potato with just the slightest bite. You can usually find the shelf-stable packaged gnocchi nestled among the dry pastas in your grocery store.

MAKES 4 SERVINGS

3 tablespoons extra-virgin olive oil
2 large shallots, thinly sliced
1 (1-pound) package shelf-stable gnocchi
3 medium cloves garlic, minced
¼ cup dry white wine
5 ounces baby spinach
⅓ cup oil-packed sun-dried tomatoes, drained and coarsely chopped

1 (15-ounce) can cannellini or great northern beans, drained and rinsed
1 tablespoon balsamic vinegar
Kosher salt and freshly ground black pepper
Pinch of red pepper flakes
¼ cup (about ¾ ounce) shredded Parmesan cheese

1 Heat the oil in a 10-inch skillet over medium heat. Add the shallots and cook until just starting to soften, about 3 minutes. Add the gnocchi and continue to cook, stirring gently, until starting to crisp, 4 to 5 minutes. Stir in the garlic and cook for 1 minute. Deglaze the pan with the wine, scraping up any browned bits in the bottom of the skillet with a wooden spoon.

2 Add the spinach a handful at a time, gently stirring until wilted, 2 to 3 minutes. Add the tomatoes and beans and cook until heated through, 2 to 3 minutes. Splash with the vinegar and season to taste with salt, pepper, and red pepper flakes. Top with the cheese before serving.

TIP: Don't be tempted to cook the gnocchi in boiling water before you add it to the skillet. Go straight from the package to the pan—you'll be pleasantly surprised!

KIMCHI FRIED RICE
with Enoki Mushrooms and Tofu

If you're looking for something that's quick, easy, filling, and packed with flavor, look no further. Bonus points: it's pretty darn healthy too! Brown rice is stir-fried with kimchi, tofu, and mushrooms for a super-savory and hearty supper. In my family, we put eggs on top of everything, and this dish is no exception. Before you cook up your rice, heat a tablespoon of sesame oil in your skillet over medium heat, fry up a few eggs, then set them aside while you cook dinner. When the rice is piping hot, place a fried egg on top of each serving and you're good to go! If you're not a fan of precooked packaged rice (I will openly admit that I love the stuff), you can use about 1 cup of leftover cooked rice. Just make sure that your rice has been hanging out in the fridge for a day or two, otherwise it will turn to mush.

MAKES 4 SERVINGS

3 tablespoons unsalted butter
1 small yellow onion, diced
8 ounces enoki mushrooms, roots removed, rinsed and drained
2 cups kimchi
½ (12-ounce) package extra-firm tofu, drained and diced

1 (8-ounce) package precooked brown rice
2 tablespoons soy sauce, or to taste
1 tablespoon sesame oil
3 green onions, white and green parts thinly sliced
Toasted sesame seeds, for serving

1   Melt the butter in a 10-inch skillet over medium-low heat. Add the onions and mushrooms and cook until soft, about 5 minutes. Stir in the kimchi and tofu and continue to cook until warmed through, about 3 minutes.
2   Break up the rice into the skillet and gently stir to incorporate. Season with the soy sauce and sesame oil. Increase the heat to medium and cook, stirring, until the rice has absorbed the sauce and is hot, 3 to 5 minutes. Let the rice sit undisturbed for another 2 to 3 minutes to brown slightly on the bottom.
3   Divide the fried rice between four bowls. Sprinkle with the green onions and sesame seeds before serving.

SWAP IT OUT: No enoki? No problem. You can swap out the enoki mushrooms with stemmed and sliced oyster mushrooms or even sliced white button mushrooms.

PASTA E CECI
(Italian Pasta and Chickpea Stew)

This is one of my favorite "Oh shoot, I forgot to plan something for dinner" meals. It comes together super quick (even with three kids sitting around the kitchen island trying to finish homework, the dog needing to be let outside, and who knows what else going on). The best part is that it tastes divine. Just a few simple ingredients (beans, pasta, tomatoes, and broth) combine into an ultra-comforting and ultra-filling dish with almost everything grabbed from the pantry. You can really throw in any type of dried pasta you have in the cupboard, and no one will be the wiser. For the best flavor, use a really nice aged balsamic vinegar (think syrup-like) to finish the dish. Don't forget to smash some of the chickpeas before adding them to the soup: it helps to create a thick and creamy broth.

MAKES 4 SERVINGS

1 (15-ounce) can chickpeas, rinsed and drained
2 tablespoons extra-virgin olive oil, plus more for serving
1 small yellow onion, finely chopped
3 medium cloves garlic, minced
1 sprig fresh rosemary, or ½ teaspoon dried
Pinch of red pepper flakes
Kosher salt and freshly ground black pepper

1 (15-ounce) can diced tomatoes
3 cups vegetable or chicken broth, divided
1 cup ditalini pasta
1 small bunch lacinato kale (about 7 ounces), tough stems removed and leaves shredded
¼ cup chopped fresh basil
1 tablespoon aged balsamic vinegar
Shredded pecorino cheese, for serving

1   In a small bowl, smash about ½ cup of the chickpeas, then combine with the remaining chickpeas and set aside.
2   Heat the oil in a 10-inch skillet over medium heat. Add the onions to the skillet and cook until the onions are soft, about 5 minutes. Stir in the garlic, rosemary, and red pepper flakes and cook for 1 minute. Season to taste with salt and pepper.
3   Stir in the tomatoes and 2 cups of the broth. Bring to a boil. Stir in the pasta, reduce heat, and simmer, covered, stirring frequently until the pasta is just al dente, about 8 minutes. Stir in the kale, chickpeas, and the remaining 1 cup broth. Continue to cook until the kale is wilted and the chickpeas are warmed through, about 5 minutes. Remove the rosemary sprig. Stir in the basil and vinegar and season to taste with salt and pepper.
4   Ladle into four bowls and top with the cheese and an extra drizzle of olive oil.

ORZO

with Asparagus, Peas, and Parmesan

Talk about a celebration of spring! Asparagus, peas, spinach, and basil make this orzo go from simple side dish to straight-up dinner. Sprinkle some lemon zest and Parmesan on top (or rather, stirred in, if you're getting technical), and this is a showstopper of a meal. But you know what? It's actually surprisingly quick and easy to make. If asparagus isn't in season, you can swap it out with blanched green beans or broccoli. Still green, still delicious, and still super simple to prepare.

MAKES 4 SERVINGS

2 tablespoons unsalted butter

1 bunch (about 30) thin asparagus spears, tough ends removed and stalks sliced 1 inch long on the diagonal

5 ounces baby spinach

3 medium cloves garlic, minced

Kosher salt and freshly ground black pepper

1¾ cups vegetable or chicken broth

1 tablespoon freshly squeezed lemon juice

2 teaspoons fresh lemon zest

1 cup orzo

1 cup (about 3 ounces) shredded Parmesan cheese

1 cup fresh or frozen and thawed peas

2 tablespoons chopped fresh basil

1   Melt the butter in a 10-inch skillet over medium heat. Add the asparagus and cook until crisp-tender, 2 to 4 minutes. Add the spinach a handful at a time, gently stirring until wilted, another 2 to 4 minutes. Stir in the garlic and cook until fragrant, about 1 minute. Season to taste with salt and pepper. Transfer the asparagus mixture from the skillet to a large plate or bowl.

2   Add the broth, lemon juice, and lemon zest to your skillet and bring to a boil. Add the orzo to the skillet and reduce the heat to medium-low. Simmer, covered, until most of the liquid is absorbed and the orzo is tender, about 10 minutes, stirring a few times.

3   Stir in the cheese, peas, and basil. Fold in the asparagus mixture, with the juices. Serve immediately.

TIP: If you want to add a bit of protein to this dish, stir in ½ cup of toasted sliced almonds right before serving. Not only are they a healthy fat with a kick of vegetarian protein, they also add a delightful crunch to the dish.

CAULIFLOWER AND EGGPLANT MASALA

For me, masala is a tomatoey, creamy comfort food. It's flavorfully spicy, not hot spicy, so it appeals to all of the eaters in my house. Compared to the more commonly known curry powder, garam masala (also a mix of spices, like curry) has a sweeter, warmer flavor than curry's more spicy and earthy kick. The cauliflower and eggplant reach that just-tender balance where you can smoosh them with your fork, but they won't slide off when you're ready to take a bite. Sometimes I'll add cubed paneer or tofu when I mix in the peas. This is one of those dishes that tastes great the first day but really comes together the next, when the flavors have a chance to get to know each other. You can keep this dish vegan by using coconut milk, or tiptoe into the animal kingdom with a bit of heavy cream.

MAKES 4 TO 6 SERVINGS

2 tablespoons high-heat oil, such as canola or safflower
1 small yellow onion, thinly sliced
3 medium cloves garlic, minced
2 tablespoons tomato paste
1 tablespoon garam masala
2 teaspoons minced peeled fresh ginger
½ teaspoon ground turmeric
1 small head cauliflower (about 1 pound), cut into 1-inch florets
1 medium eggplant (about ½ pound), cut into 1-inch cubes

Kosher salt and freshly ground black pepper
1 (15-ounce) can tomato sauce
1 cup vegetable broth or water
1 cup frozen peas, thawed
½ cup heavy cream or full-fat unsweetened coconut milk
¼ cup chopped fresh cilantro
Freshly squeezed lemon juice
Naan bread, for serving

1 Heat the oil in a 10-inch skillet over medium heat. Add the onions and cook until soft, about 5 minutes. Stir in the garlic, tomato paste, garam masala, ginger, and turmeric; cook until fragrant, about 1 minute.

2 Add the cauliflower and eggplant and toss to coat with the spices. Season to taste with salt and pepper. Pour in the tomato sauce and broth. Bring to a boil, then reduce to a simmer. Cook, covered, until the cauliflower and eggplant are tender, stirring often, about 20 minutes.

3 Stir in the peas, heavy cream, and cilantro and heat through, about 5 minutes. Season to taste with the lemon juice, salt, and pepper. Serve with naan bread for dipping.

THAI GREEN CURRY

with Tofu and Rice Cakes

Moment of truth: I used to scoff at those precooked packages of rice in the grocery store. Why in the world would you buy prepared rice when it is so darn easy to cook? You know why? Because that's one less pot to clean and twenty minutes of your life back. That prepared rice also turns into delightfully crisp rice cakes, pan-seared in your skillet, then topped with a creamy, vibrant, and flavorful green curry sauce loaded with veggies and soft tofu. I like red bell peppers for both their color and flavor, but there's no reason not to use green, orange, or yellow. This dish is also a great way to use up any leftover veggies in your fridge. Steamed sliced carrots, sauteed onions or eggplant, or almost anything else you can think of is a great addition to or substitution in this meal.

MAKES 4 SERVINGS

2 (8-ounce) packages precooked basmati or jasmine rice

1 large egg, lightly beaten

2 tablespoons all-purpose or rice flour

2 tablespoons high-heat oil, such as canola or safflower, divided

8 ounces green beans, trimmed and cut into 2-inch lengths

1 red bell pepper, chopped

1 (8-ounce) can sliced bamboo shoots, drained

1 (14-ounce) can full-fat unsweetened coconut milk

2 to 3 tablespoons Thai green curry paste

2 tablespoons soy sauce

1 tablespoon packed dark brown sugar

1 (12-ounce) package extra-firm tofu, drained and cut into 1-inch cubes

¼ cup fresh Thai basil leaves

2 tablespoons freshly squeezed lime juice

Lime wedges, for serving

1   Preheat the oven to 200 degrees F.

2   Microwave the rice to warm, about 90 seconds. Using a pastry cutter or knife on a cutting board, smash or chop about half of the rice until coarsely chopped. Combine with the remaining rice and stir in the egg and flour. Using wet hands, form the rice mixture into eight 3-inch-wide cakes.

3   Heat 1 tablespoon of the oil in a 10-inch skillet over medium heat. Working in batches, carefully lay the rice cakes in the pan and cook until golden brown on both sides, about 6 minutes total. Transfer the cakes to a baking sheet and keep warm in the oven.

→

4   Add the remaining 1 tablespoon oil to the skillet over medium heat. Add the green beans, peppers, and bamboo shoots and cook until tender and starting to brown, stirring occasionally, about 7 minutes.

5   Whisk together the coconut milk, curry paste to taste, soy sauce, and brown sugar in a small bowl. Pour over the green bean mixture. Gently stir in the tofu and bring to a simmer. Partially cover and cook until the tofu is warmed through and the green beans are tender, about 7 minutes. Remove from the heat and stir in the basil and lime juice. Serve the curry over the rice cakes with lime wedges on the side for squeezing.

TIP: Second moment of truth—green curry is possibly one of my favorite dishes to eat. But if you find you're not going through your curry paste fast enough, you can dollop it by the tablespoonful onto parchment paper, freeze it, then store it in the freezer in a resealable plastic bag for several months.

FRENCH ONION SOUP-STRATA

Any excuse to sink into a piping hot bowl of French onion soup is good enough for me. And this recipe is no exception. It's all of the best things about French onion soup: caramelized sweet onions, crusty sourdough bread, aromatic thyme, and sweet sherry, all smothered in earthy Gruyère cheese. But without the soup. This traditional soup has been turned into a savory bread pudding, and it couldn't be more satisfying or cozier to eat. Serve it for breakfast with fresh fruit or for dinner with a crisp green salad.

MAKES 4 TO 6 SERVINGS

6 large eggs
1½ cups whole milk
2 tablespoons Dijon mustard
1 tablespoon Worcestershire sauce
Kosher salt and freshly ground black
  pepper
1 day-old sourdough bread loaf (about
  1 pound), cut into 1-inch cubes
3 tablespoons unsalted butter, plus more
  for the skillet

2 large sweet onions, thinly sliced
4 medium cloves garlic, minced
1 teaspoon chopped fresh thyme, or
  ¼ teaspoon dried
¼ cup dry sherry
½ cup dry white wine
2 cups (about 6 ounces) shredded
  Gruyère cheese, divided

1 Preheat the oven to 350 degrees F.
2 In a large bowl, whisk together the eggs, milk, mustard, and Worcestershire sauce. Season to taste with salt and pepper. Fold in the sourdough bread cubes and let them soak, gently stirring on occasion, while you prepare the onions.
3 Melt the butter in a 10-inch skillet over medium-low heat. Add the onions and cook, stirring often, until a deep golden brown, about 25 minutes. Stir in the garlic and thyme and cook until fragrant, about 1 minute. Season to taste with salt and pepper. Increase the heat to medium and add the sherry and wine. Cook until the liquid has almost evaporated, about 4 minutes.
4 Transfer the onion mixture from the skillet to a large plate or bowl. Rub the skillet with additional butter.
5 Add half of the soaked bread to the skillet and top with half of the onions and half of the cheese. Layer the remaining bread on top and drizzle with any remaining egg mixture. Scatter with the remaining onions and cheese. Transfer to the oven and bake until the bread is crisp and the custard is just set, 40 to 50 minutes. Let cool for 10 minutes before serving.

TIP: If you don't happen to have sherry on hand, you can simply replace it with more white wine or a splash of brandy.

PISTO MANCHEGO
(Spanish Ratatouille)

It's part vegetable stew, part ratatouille (a French Provençal dish of stewed veggies), and part shakshuka (a North African dish of eggs poached in a tomato, pepper, and olive oil sauce). Eggplant, zucchini, and peppers are gently simmered in a garlicky-herby tomato sauce until fork-tender, then eggs are poached directly in the sauce. The whole thing is smothered in cheese, and voilà! The best darn breakfast-brunch-dinner-what-have-you is ready. Hailing from Spain, it might seem sacrilegious to serve this with a croissant, but you'll want to sop up every last bit of sauce. Though if you have a baguette on hand, that will work too. And I know it seems like a lot of olive oil, but use it all—the eggplant absorbs it like a sponge.

MAKES 4 SERVINGS

¼ cup extra-virgin olive oil
1 small yellow onion, diced
1 small yellow bell pepper, diced
1 medium eggplant (about ½ pound), diced
1 small zucchini (about 5 ounces), diced
3 medium cloves garlic, minced
2 tablespoons chopped fresh oregano, or 2 teaspoons dried
Kosher salt and freshly ground black pepper

½ cup dry white wine
1 (15-ounce) can tomato sauce
2 tablespoons chopped fresh basil
1 to 2 tablespoons sherry or balsamic vinegar
4 large eggs (optional)
¼ cup (about 1 ounce) shredded Manchego cheese
4 croissants, for serving

1   Heat the oil in a 10-inch skillet over medium heat. Add the onions and peppers and cook until softened, stirring occasionally, about 5 minutes. Add the eggplant and zucchini and cook until softened, stirring occasionally, about 10 minutes. Stir in the garlic and oregano and cook until fragrant, about 30 seconds. Season to taste with salt and pepper.

2   Pour in the wine and simmer, stirring occasionally, until the wine is reduced by half, about 3 minutes.

3   Add the tomato sauce and bring to a simmer. Simmer gently, covered, until the juices have thickened and the vegetables are tender, about 15 minutes. Stir in the basil and vinegar to taste.

4   Use a large spoon to create four small wells in the sauce. Crack an egg into each well. Cover the pan and cook until the eggs are done to your liking, 5 to 8 minutes. Sprinkle with the cheese and serve with the croissants.

HARISSA CHICKPEAS

with Eggs and Chard

Chickpeas and rainbow chard are cooked together in a spiced and spicy mix, then scrambled with a few eggs. At its core, this is basically a super-fancy, somewhat-unusual scrambled egg dish. That's then turned into a sandwich (of sorts) by tucking the whole thing into a tortilla and forming a very unconventional burrito. There are two important things to consider when preparing this dish: One, make sure you cook the chard stems with the shallots, otherwise they will be unpleasantly crunchy. Two, harissa is a bit like a chili pesto, made with roasted peppers, garlic, spices, and olive oil all blended together to smooth, spicy perfection. Spiciness varies, so start with some, add a little more, then pile it on top of your burrito to your heart's content.

MAKES 4 SERVINGS

2 tablespoons extra-virgin olive oil
1 large shallot, thinly sliced
1 large bunch rainbow chard (about ½ pound), stems and leaves sliced, divided
2 medium cloves garlic, minced
1 teaspoon ground cumin
1 teaspoon ground coriander
2 to 3 teaspoons harissa sauce, plus more for serving

1 (15-ounce) can chickpeas, rinsed and drained
½ cup vegetable broth or water
Kosher salt and freshly ground black pepper
4 large eggs, lightly beaten
4 (10-inch) flour (white or whole wheat) tortillas
1 small English cucumber, sliced
Plain Greek yogurt, for serving

1   Heat the oil in a 10-inch skillet over medium heat. Add the shallots and chard stems and cook until softened, 5 to 7 minutes. Stir in the garlic, cumin, and coriander and cook until fragrant, about 1 minute. Add the harissa and cook for 30 seconds.

2   Stir in the chickpeas and broth and bring to a simmer. Add the chard leaves and cook, covered, until the leaves are soft, 5 to 7 minutes. Season to taste with salt and pepper. Using the back of a wooden spoon, lightly mash one-quarter of the chickpeas. Continue to cook, uncovered, until the liquid has evaporated, 2 to 4 minutes more.

3   Reduce the heat to medium-low and pour in the eggs. Let cook, stirring occasionally so that eggs are evenly distributed throughout the chickpea mixture. As the eggs set, gently stir the ingredients with a wooden spoon and scrape the bottom of the skillet. Repeat, stirring gently, until the eggs are fluffy and cooked through, 3 to 4 minutes total. Season to taste with salt and pepper.

4   Serve the mixture wrapped in the tortillas, layered with the cucumbers, and dolloped with the yogurt. Top with additional harissa sauce if you want more heat.

THREE-BEAN TAMALE PIE

We call this meal "the beast." It's larger than life and a little bumpy on top. It likes to bubble over when baking, so make sure to put your skillet on a sheet pan before putting it in the oven. And it may be "just" a vegetarian meal, but it is hearty and filling AF. If you can't find a can of three-bean blend, pick and choose two of your favorite beans (red kidney, pinto, or black bean) for a two-bean tamale pie. Heck, in a pinch, you can even make it a one-bean tamale pie, and it will be just as yummy and satisfying. Using fire-roasted tomatoes gives this dish a bit of a smoky edge. Poblano peppers are only mildly spicy, but if you're worried about heat, you can swap out the poblano with an additional bell pepper.

MAKES 6 SERVINGS

For the filling
2 tablespoons high-heat oil, such as canola or safflower
1 small yellow onion, diced
1 medium red bell pepper, diced
1 medium poblano pepper, diced
3 medium cloves garlic, minced
2 teaspoons chili powder
1 teaspoon dried oregano
Kosher salt and freshly ground black pepper
2 (15-ounce) cans three-bean blend (red kidney, pinto, and black bean), rinsed and drained
1 (15-ounce) can fire-roasted diced tomatoes
1 cup frozen corn, thawed
1 cup vegetable broth or water
1 cup (4 ounces) shredded pepper jack cheese

For the topping
¾ cup all-purpose flour
¾ cup cornmeal
2 tablespoons chopped chives
¾ teaspoon baking powder
¾ teaspoon kosher salt
¼ teaspoon baking soda
¾ cup buttermilk
3 tablespoons high-heat oil, such as canola or safflower
1 large egg

Sour cream, for serving

1 Preheat the oven to 400 degrees F.

2 To make the filling, heat the oil in a 10-inch skillet over medium heat. Add the onions and peppers and cook until soft, about 5 minutes. Stir in the garlic, chili powder, and oregano and cook until fragrant, about 1 minute. Season to taste with salt and pepper.

3 Stir in the beans, tomatoes, corn, and broth and bring to a simmer. Reduce the heat to medium-low and cook until the mixture has thickened slightly, stirring often, 5 to 10 minutes. Remove from the heat and stir in the cheese until well combined. Season to taste with salt and pepper.

4 To make the topping, in a medium bowl, whisk together the flour, cornmeal, chives, baking powder, salt, and baking soda. In a separate bowl, whisk together the buttermilk, oil, and egg. Stir the buttermilk mixture into the flour mixture until just combined.

5 Using a large spoon, place dollops of the cornbread batter on top of the bean filling, as evenly dispersed as possible. Place the skillet on a sheet pan and transfer the skillet to the oven. Bake until a pale golden brown and a skewer inserted into the cornbread comes out clean, 20 to 25 minutes. Let cool for 15 minutes before serving with sour cream.

TIP: You can actually make your own buttermilk in a pinch. Combine ¾ cup of whole milk with a scant tablespoon of white vinegar or lemon juice. Give it a stir and let it sit for 10 minutes before using.

BLACK BEAN CHILAQUILES
with Eggs

Breakfast for dinner? This super-easy take on chilaquiles will hit the spot. Normally when making chilaquiles, you deep-fry fresh tortilla pieces in oil, then create a homemade tomato and pepper sauce that simmers away for hours. I cheat a bit and make a quick sauce from canned tomatoes with chilies and boost the flavor with spices. Instead of frying my own tortillas, I simply grab a bag of chips. The whole thing is topped off with eggs and black beans for a powerhouse of a meal. If you don't have black beans on hand, pinto or red kidney beans make an excellent substitute. Choose the tomatoes and chilies' heat level based on your spice preference—mild, medium, or hot AF.

MAKES 4 SERVINGS

1 tablespoon high-heat oil, such as canola or safflower

1 small red onion, thinly sliced

3 medium cloves garlic, minced

½ teaspoon ground cumin

½ teaspoon ground coriander

½ teaspoon dried oregano

2 (10-ounce) cans diced tomatoes with chilies

1 (15-ounce) can black beans, rinsed and drained

½ cup vegetable or chicken broth

Kosher salt and freshly ground black pepper

1 (8-ounce) bag corn tortilla chips

4 large eggs

1 large firm-ripe avocado, halved, pitted, and sliced

½ cup Mexican crema or sour cream

Lime wedges, for serving

1   Preheat the oven to 425 degrees F.

2   Heat the oil in a 10-inch skillet over medium heat. Add the onions and cook until softened, about 5 minutes. Stir in the garlic, cumin, coriander, and oregano and cook until fragrant, about 1 minute. Pour in the tomatoes and their juices, beans, and broth and bring to a simmer. Cook, stirring occasionally, until the liquid has thickened slightly, about 5 minutes. Season to taste with salt and pepper.

3   Stir the tortilla chips into the sauce, breaking a few up as needed, to coat. With the back of a large spoon, create four wells in the sauce. Crack an egg into each well and season with salt and pepper. Transfer the skillet to the oven and bake until the whites are set and the yolks are cooked to your liking, 9 to 11 minutes.

4   Carefully remove the skillet from the oven and portion the chilaquiles onto plates. Serve with the avocado slices, crema, and lime wedges.

TIP: You can cook this entire dish on the stove top, if you prefer. Instead of baking the eggs in the oven, you can crack the eggs into the simmering sauce, cover the dish, and poach the eggs to your preferred doneness.

A FISH OUT OF WATER:

Seafood Recipes

Fish is versatile. Both in how you can buy it and how you can prepare it. Fresh fish, canned fish, frozen fish, shellfish . . . We are diving into deep waters here (see what I just did?). Fish can be fancy when dressed up (Pan-Seared Salmon with Braised Lentil Salad, page 55), simple when dressed down (Tuna Noodle Skillet Casserole with Peas and Prosciutto, page 82), comforting when dressed with the expected (Skillet Shrimp "Boil" with Potatoes, Corn, and Sausage, page 59), and fun when dressed in new clothes (Thai Red Curry Rice with Halibut, page 63).

You'll find these recipes to be most forgiving (as in easy to prepare and cook) but never lacking in flavor or fun. That's why I love seafood. Oh, I also love seafood because it tastes great and is good for you. Fish and shellfish are high in protein, low in fat, and packed full of omega-3 fatty acids and vitamins. If you feel that your fillet may break the bank, play around with different types of fish in these recipes. Though fresh fillets are best, don't fear frozen fish or shellfish—you can often get more bang for your buck and don't have to worry about going to the grocery store the same day you are preparing your meal.

BAKED COD

with Artichokes, Sun-Dried Tomatoes, and Olives

It's amazing how bright and fresh a meal can taste when it's actually made mostly with ingredients found jarred in your cupboard. I may not be selling the dish with that description, but I bet you'll be surprised at the results. Canned artichoke hearts, sun-dried tomatoes, and Castelvetrano olives bring a surprising pop of both color and flavor after being roasted in a superhot oven. Both the veggies and the fish get an extra boost from the leftover tomato oil (waste not, want not, I say!), and the whole thing is relatively hands-off, except for a few quick stirs. This dish is equally at home as a quick weeknight dinner between grocery store runs or a fancy night of entertaining on the patio.

MAKES 4 SERVINGS

4 (6-ounce) skinless cod fillets, about 1 to 1½ inches thick

Kosher salt and freshly ground black pepper

2 (14-ounce) cans quartered artichoke hearts, drained

1 small yellow onion, thickly sliced

¾ cup oil-packed sun-dried tomatoes, drained (¼ cup oil reserved)

½ cup pitted Castelvetrano olives, halved

3 medium cloves garlic, minced

2 teaspoons fresh lemon zest

2 tablespoons freshly squeezed lemon juice

2 tablespoons chopped fresh mint

1   Preheat the oven to 450 degrees F.

2   Pat the cod dry with paper towels and season with salt and pepper. Set aside.

3   In a 10-inch skillet, toss together the artichoke hearts and onions with 2 tablespoons of the reserved tomato oil; season with salt and pepper. Roast in the oven until lightly browned, about 25 minutes, stirring halfway through roasting.

4   Carefully remove the skillet from the oven and reduce the temperature to 425 degrees F.

5   Stir the sun-dried tomatoes, olives, garlic, lemon zest, and 1 tablespoon of the tomato oil into the artichoke mixture. Nestle the cod on top of the artichoke mixture and brush with the remaining 1 tablespoon tomato oil. Bake until the fish flakes apart when gently pressed with your finger or reaches an internal temperature of 140 degrees F, about 15 minutes.

6   Carefully remove the skillet from the oven. Drizzle with the lemon juice and sprinkle with the mint before serving.

SWAP IT OUT: You can use haddock or mahi mahi fillets instead of cod.

PAN-SEARED SALMON

with Braised Lentil Salad

I like to file this dish under "fancy comfort food." It comes off pretty sophisticated: a rich and flavorful dish of lentils braised in aromatics with pops of tangy goat cheese, topped with golden-crusted salmon. But at its core, it's a simple warm bean dish topped with a nice piece of fish. Because the salmon is kept so simple, make sure you buy the best-quality fish you can find. You really want to experience the rich, fatty flavors of fresh-caught wild salmon (think king and coho), not bottom-of-the-barrel salmon (no offense, chum and Atlantic). In a pinch, frozen fillets are also an excellent choice. For the best look and "mouthfeel" (that is, how the braised lentils feel in your mouth when you eat them), take the time to mince the onions, carrots, and celery superfine so they are about the same size as the lentils.

MAKES 4 SERVINGS

2 tablespoons unsalted butter
3 tablespoons high-heat oil, such as canola or safflower, divided
2 medium ribs celery, finely chopped
1 large carrot, finely chopped
1 small yellow onion, finely chopped
3 medium cloves garlic, minced
1 teaspoon chopped fresh thyme, or ¼ teaspoon dried

Kosher salt and freshly ground black pepper
3 cups chicken or vegetable broth
1 cup green lentils, picked over and rinsed
5 ounces baby spinach
1 tablespoon freshly squeezed lemon juice
4 (6-ounce) center-cut, skin-on salmon fillets, about 1½ inches thick
4 ounces fresh goat cheese, crumbled

1 Melt the butter and 1 tablespoon of the oil over medium heat in a 10-inch skillet. Add the celery, carrots, and onions. Cook, stirring often, until soft and just starting to brown, about 7 minutes. Add the garlic and thyme and cook until fragrant, about 1 minute. Season to taste with salt and pepper. Stir in the broth and lentils and bring to a boil. Reduce the heat to low and cook, covered, until the lentils are tender, 25 to 30 minutes, stirring occasionally.

2 Uncover and cook, stirring often, until most of the liquid has evaporated, about 2 minutes. Stir in the spinach a handful at a time and cook until wilted, 3 to 5 minutes. Mix in the lemon juice and season again with salt and pepper. Transfer to a large bowl and cover to keep warm.

3 Pat the salmon dry with paper towels and season with salt and pepper.

4 Wipe out the skillet with a paper towel if necessary. Heat the remaining 2 tablespoons oil over medium heat in your skillet. Carefully lay the salmon, skin side up, in the skillet. Cook until browned, 4 to 6 minutes. Flip the salmon over and cook until the desired doneness is reached, 3 to 6 minutes for medium.

5 Fold the goat cheese into the lentil mixture. Serve the salmon over the lentils.

BROWN BUTTER HALIBUT

with Celeriac

Your first question is probably, "What the heck is a celeriac?" Also known as celery root, celeriac is a type of celery that's grown for its root instead of its stalks. It tastes a bit like a parsnip, is often cooked like a potato, and looks like an alien from another planet. When I mentioned the potato bit to my tween, he asked me, "So this is fancy fish and chips, then?" If you consider halibut cooked in brown butter, then poached along with celeriac, capers, white wine, and shallots to be the equivalent of fish and chips, then . . . yes. This is *really* fancy fish and chips. It can be tricky to brown butter in a dark cast iron skillet, so follow your nose. When you start to smell a sweet and nutty aroma, you know you're there. Don't let it go too long, otherwise you risk burning your butter and will need to start over.

MAKES 4 SERVINGS

4 (6-ounce) skinless halibut fillets, about 1 inch thick
Kosher salt and freshly ground black pepper
4 tablespoons unsalted butter
1 large celeriac (about 1 pound), peeled and cut into ¼-inch cubes
3 medium shallots, halved and thinly sliced

3 medium cloves garlic, minced
3 tablespoons capers, rinsed and drained
1 cup dry white wine
2 tablespoons chopped fresh parsley
1 tablespoon freshly squeezed lemon juice
Lemon wedges, for serving
Crusty bread, for serving (optional)

1   Pat the halibut dry with paper towels and season with salt and pepper.
2   Melt the butter over medium heat in a 10-inch skillet. Place the halibut, skin side up, in the skillet and cook until the butter begins to brown, 3 to 4 minutes. Gently remove the halibut with a spatula and transfer to a plate.
3   Add the celeriac and shallots to your skillet. Cook until just softened, about 5 minutes. Stir in the garlic and capers and cook for 1 minute. Season to taste with salt and pepper. Add the wine and bring to a gentle simmer. Place the halibut, skin side down, on top of the vegetables. Cook, covered, at a gentle simmer over medium-low heat until the halibut flakes apart when gently pressed with your finger and becomes opaque or reaches an internal temperature of 135 degrees F, about 7 minutes. Gently transfer the halibut to a warmed serving platter or individual shallow bowls.
4   Bring the remaining liquid and vegetables in your skillet to a boil over high heat. Cook until the sauce is thick, about 2 minutes. Remove from the heat and stir in the parsley and lemon juice. Season with additional salt and pepper.
5   Drizzle the sauce over the fish and serve the celeriac alongside. Serve with the lemon wedges for squeezing and the crusty bread.

SWAP IT OUT: Don't have halibut or it's too pricey? Try cod, tilapia, or haddock.

SKILLET SHRIMP "BOIL"

with Potatoes, Corn, and Sausage

A tamer version of its famous backyard cousin, the low-country boil, this dish features all of the same flavors as the original but with half the work and half the mess. Caramelized potatoes, sweet corn, smoky sausage, and plump shrimp are roasted with everyone's favorite seasoning for a taste of a southeastern outdoor feast. Oh, there's also quite a bit of butter because . . . well, it's delicious. Once the whole thing is ready, instead of tossing dinner out on your newspapers like a low-country boil, you can eat this dish from a shallow bowl and save the newspapers for after-dinner reading.

MAKES 4 SERVINGS

2 tablespoons unsalted butter, at room temperature

1 teaspoon Old Bay Seasoning

1 teaspoon freshly squeezed lemon juice

½ pound baby Dutch or red potatoes, halved if small, quartered if large

2 andouille sausages, sliced 1 inch thick

1 tablespoon high-heat oil, such as canola or safflower

Kosher salt and freshly ground black pepper

1 pound peeled and deveined shrimp, tails removed

1 cup fresh or frozen and thawed corn

2 tablespoons chopped fresh parsley

Lemon wedges, for serving

1 Preheat the oven to 500 degrees F with the rack positioned in the lower third of the oven.

2 In a small bowl, combine the butter, Old Bay, and lemon juice. Set aside.

3 In a 10-inch skillet, toss the potatoes and sausage with the oil; season to taste with salt and pepper. Roast in the oven until the potatoes are lightly browned and tender, 25 to 30 minutes, stirring occasionally.

4 Season the shrimp with salt and pepper.

5 Carefully remove the skillet from the oven and reduce the temperature to 425 degrees F. Add the shrimp, corn, and 1 tablespoon of the butter mixture to your skillet. Toss the ingredients to combine and return the skillet to the oven. Roast until the shrimp are opaque and cooked through, 6 to 8 minutes.

6 Carefully remove the skillet from the oven and toss the shrimp mixture with the remaining butter mixture and the parsley. Serve immediately with the lemon wedges for squeezing.

TIP: Can't find Old Bay Seasoning? You can make your own simpler version by combining 2 teaspoons celery salt, 1½ teaspoons dry mustard, 1½ teaspoons ground black pepper, 1 teaspoon smoked paprika, ½ teaspoon ground nutmeg, ½ teaspoon ground ginger, and a pinch each of cloves, cardamom, and allspice. Store in an airtight container in a cool, dry cupboard for up to 6 months.

CLAM FIDEOS

It's the age-old question: Which came first, the noodle or the dish? Fideos is both a type of noodle and a soup. The noodles are short, round, and stick-like (similar to broken angel hair pasta or spaghetti), and the soup can range from, well . . . soupy to thick. I've split the difference in texture for my take on this classic Spanish dish. Since the noodles cook in the broth mixture, they absorb most of the liquid (and the flavor) while leaving just enough juiciness behind to slurp up once you reach the bottom of the bowl. The smoky flavor and spice level will vary from mild to hot, depending on how much paprika you use. You can easily substitute fresh mussels or peeled and deveined shrimp for the clams, depending on what you can find at the supermarket.

MAKES 4 SERVINGS

6 ounces fideos noodles or angel hair pasta, broken into 1- to 2-inch lengths
3 tablespoons extra-virgin olive oil, divided
1 medium fennel bulb (about 8 ounces), trimmed, cored, and thinly sliced
1 small yellow onion, finely chopped
Kosher salt and freshly ground black pepper
3 medium cloves garlic, minced
1 tablespoon tomato paste

1 to 1½ teaspoons smoked paprika
1 (15-ounce) can fire-roasted tomatoes, drained and juices reserved
2¼ cups chicken or vegetable broth
¼ cup dry white wine
1 pound Manila or littleneck clams, cleaned (see tip)
¼ cup roughly chopped fresh parsley
Lemon wedges, for serving

1   In a 10-inch skillet, toss the pasta with 1 tablespoon of the oil. Toast over medium heat, stirring often, until browned and nutty smelling, 3 to 5 minutes. Transfer to a large bowl or plate.

2   Add the remaining 2 tablespoons oil to your skillet over medium heat. Add the fennel and onions and cook until softened and beginning to brown, 7 to 9 minutes. Season to taste with salt and pepper. Stir in the garlic, tomato paste, and paprika and cook until fragrant, about 1 minute. Add the tomatoes, without their juices, and cook until the mixture is somewhat dry, 2 to 3 minutes.

3   Add the broth, wine, and reserved tomato juice to your skillet. Bring to a boil and carefully stir in the toasted pasta. Reduce to a simmer and cook, uncovered, stirring occasionally, for 8 minutes. Add the clams, and continue to cook, covered, until the pasta is al dente and the clams open, 2 to 3 minutes more. Discard any unopened clams. Stir in the parsley. Let cool for 5 minutes before serving with the lemon wedges for squeezing.

TIP: Sometimes clams and mussels can have a bit of grit (sand) inside them. Before cooking shellfish, soak them in a large bowl of cool, clean water for 20 minutes. Drain and rinse, and they are ready to be used in your recipe.

THAI RED CURRY RICE
with Halibut

The flavors and colors of this dish are bright and bold: red curry paste, bell peppers, and fresh herbs. But it is somehow simultaneously super comforting and warming, thanks to all of that coconut milk and rice. Play around with how much red curry paste you add: If you like it mild, start with a tablespoon. If you like to spice things up, add a touch more. I always opt to spend a bit more money on fresh halibut, but if you're just looking for a cheap weeknight dinner, it's perfectly acceptable to buy frozen cod.

MAKES 4 SERVINGS

1 (14-ounce) can unsweetened coconut milk

1 to 2 tablespoons red curry paste

4 (6-ounce) skinless halibut fillets, about 1 inch thick

Kosher salt and freshly ground black pepper

1 tablespoon sesame oil

2 medium red or yellow bell peppers, finely diced

4 green onions, white and green parts separated and thinly sliced

2 teaspoons minced peeled fresh ginger

2 medium cloves garlic, minced

1 cup long-grain white rice, such as jasmine or basmati

1¼ cups chicken or vegetable broth

½ cup unsalted roasted peanuts

2 tablespoons chopped fresh Thai or regular basil leaves

Lime wedges, for serving

1   In a small bowl, whisk together the coconut milk and red curry paste until smooth; set aside.

2   Pat the halibut dry with paper towels and season with salt and pepper; set aside.

3   Heat the oil over medium heat in a 10-inch skillet. Add the peppers and green onion whites and cook, stirring often, until the peppers soften, about 5 minutes. Stir in the ginger and garlic and cook until fragrant, about 1 minute more. Add the rice and cook until the edges start to turn translucent, about 1 minute. Stir in 1 cup of the curry sauce, all of the broth, and a generous pinch of salt. Bring to a boil.

4   Carefully place the halibut, skin side down, on top of the rice mixture. Drizzle with a little bit of the curry sauce. Reduce the heat to a simmer and cook, covered, until the liquid is absorbed by the rice and the halibut easily flakes apart when gently pressed with your finger, 12 to 15 minutes.

5   Remove the skillet from the heat. Sprinkle the rice with the remaining green onions, the peanuts, and basil. Drizzle with the remaining curry sauce to taste over the fish and rice and serve with the lime wedges for squeezing.

SCALLOP ORZOTTO

with Fennel, Orange, and Goat Cheese

"Orzotto" is a play on words: it's where orzo pasta meets risotto rice, making for a creamy and comforting pasta-grain-type dish, but requiring less time and less stirring. We consider this one of our "fancy" dinners in our house, even though it's so easy to make. The dish is somewhat exotic (thanks to scallops), creamy (thanks to goat cheese), fresh (thanks to orange zest and juice), and unusual (thanks to thyme). No one needs to know that scallops cook within literal minutes, and orzo takes just a bit longer than that (but not by much), and fennel is just a root vegetable. Let's keep the power of this easy dish a secret so that we can still impress, shall we?

MAKES 4 SERVINGS

12 ounces sea scallops

Kosher salt and freshly ground black pepper

2 tablespoons extra-virgin olive oil, plus more as needed

1 medium fennel bulb (about 8 ounces), trimmed, cored, and thinly sliced

½ small red onion, thinly sliced

2 medium cloves garlic, minced

1 teaspoon chopped fresh thyme, or ¼ teaspoon dried

2¼ cups chicken or vegetable broth

1 cup orzo pasta

2 tablespoons freshly squeezed orange juice

2 teaspoons fresh orange zest

4 ounces goat cheese, crumbled

2 tablespoons sliced fresh chives

1   Pat the scallops dry with paper towels and season each side with salt and pepper.
2   Heat the oil in a 10-inch skillet over medium heat. Add the scallops and cook for 2 minutes, without touching or moving them. Flip the scallops over and cook for 1 additional minute. Transfer to a warm plate and cover loosely with aluminum foil.
3   Add the fennel and onions to your skillet and cook until tender and golden, about 10 minutes, adding a touch more oil if needed. Stir in the garlic and thyme and cook for 1 additional minute. Season to taste with salt and pepper.
4   Add the broth and bring to a simmer. Stir in the orzo, orange juice, and orange zest. Simmer, covered, over medium-low heat, stirring often, until the orzo is cooked through and most of the liquid is absorbed, 10 to 12 minutes. Remove from the heat and gently stir in the goat cheese.
5   Place the scallops back in your skillet on top of the orzo, cover, and let rest for 2 to 5 minutes to warm through. Serve the orzo topped with the scallops and sprinkled with the chives.

TIP: For the best flavor and sear, look for large scallops ("diver" or "U-20" scallops versus bay scallops) and check the packaging or ask your fishmonger to confirm that they are dry-packed (instead of soaking in a brine).

WEEKNIGHT ORZO PAELLA
with Mussels and Chorizo

You could spend hours making a traditional paella, or you could whip up something almost* as amazing in about thirty minutes. I'll let you choose . . . OK, just kidding, I'm going to choose for you. Make this super-easy and aromatic paella, and you won't be disappointed. It has all of the classic components: briny shellfish, spicy sausage, smoky paprika and tomatoes, fragrant saffron, and colorful little peas. Except it's simple to prepare, and no giant paella pan or live fire is required. This recipe also happens to be endlessly versatile and flexible. Replace the chorizo with hot Italian sausage, mild sausage, or even chicken sausage if you're not a fan of spice. Instead of mussels, you can use shrimp or clams (see the tip on cleaning fresh shellfish on page 60). You could even swap out the green peas with chopped green beans if you're so motivated. Make it your own take on the classic—it's going to be delicious no matter what.

Yes, yes, I know this isn't "traditional" paella. And, honestly, there is no substitute for the real thing cooked outdoors over an open flame. But for a quick weeknight meal, this is pretty darn good.

MAKES 4 SERVINGS

1 pound mussels
⅛ teaspoon saffron threads
¼ cup hot water
1 tablespoon extra-virgin olive oil
8 ounces cured chorizo sausage, diced
4 medium cloves garlic, minced
1 teaspoon smoked paprika

1 cup orzo pasta
1¾ cups chicken or vegetable broth
1 (15-ounce) can fire-roasted tomatoes
Kosher salt and freshly ground black pepper
1 cup frozen peas, thawed
2 tablespoons chopped fresh parsley

1   Soak the mussels in a large bowl of cold water for 20 to 30 minutes to allow them to purge any grit. Drain and rinse, gently scrubbing, if needed. Debeard the mussels by pulling the clump of hairlike fibers poking out from the side of the mussel toward the hinge of the shell (some beards are harder to remove than others). Set aside.

2   In a small bowl, submerge the saffron threads in the hot water to "bloom" (release the flavors). Set aside.

3   Heat the oil in a 10-inch skillet over medium heat. Add the sausage and cook until browned, stirring occasionally, 3 to 4 minutes. Stir in the garlic and paprika and cook until fragrant, about 30 seconds more.

→

4   Add the orzo and cook, stirring occasionally, until lightly toasted, about
    1 minute. Add the reserved saffron water, broth, and tomatoes with their juices.
    Season to taste with salt and pepper. Bring to a boil, partially cover, and reduce
    the heat to a simmer over medium-low. Cook until the orzo is almost al dente
    and the liquid is reduced by half, stirring often, about 7 minutes.
5   Stir the peas into the orzo and scatter the mussels over the top. Continue to
    cook over medium-low heat, covered, until the mussels open and the orzo
    is cooked, 3 to 5 minutes. Remove from the heat and let sit, covered, for
    5 minutes. Discard any unopened mussels, sprinkle with the parsley, and serve.

SWAP IT OUT: Saffron threads are super-duper expensive, but they are so worth it. Not only do they add floral/earthy flavor to your dish, they also add amazing color. In a pinch, instead of saffron, you can add a touch of turmeric for color.

TIP: Check out How to Pick Mussels on page 74.

GLAZED SALMON

with Black-Eyed Peas, Pomegranate Seeds, and Arugula

The trick to perfectly cooked salmon is to start with a hot-as-heck pan to sear the skin to crispy goodness, then quickly reduce the heat to cook the fish low and slow. The fish is then paired with a warm arugula salad with bursts of bright citrus, creamy black-eyed peas, and little bits of crunchy pomegranate seeds. When working with pomegranates, take caution! The seeds (technically called *arils*) will stain the living daylights out of any light-colored clothes (and your hands). Trim the top and bottom of your pomegranate with a sharp knife. Then make about six slits through the red skin into the pith, all the way around the pomegranate. Gently peel the segments apart and place them in a large bowl of water. Using your fingers, you can easily pop the seeds out of the pith and into the water. The seeds will sink and the pith will float. Remove the pith, then drain the water to gather all of the seeds.

MAKES 4 SERVINGS

1 large Cara Cara or navel orange
3 tablespoons extra-virgin olive oil
2 tablespoons balsamic vinegar
1 tablespoon Dijon mustard
1 tablespoon honey
Kosher salt and freshly ground black
   pepper

4 (6-ounce) skin-on salmon fillets, 1 to
   1½ inches thick
2 (15-ounce) cans black-eyed peas,
   drained and rinsed
1 cup pomegranate seeds
5 ounces baby arugula

1 Preheat the oven to 500 degrees F with the rack positioned in the lower third of the oven.

2 Cut the orange in half and juice one half to get 2 tablespoons of juice. Remove the peel and pith from the remaining half and cut the flesh into ½-inch pieces; set aside.

3 In a small bowl, whisk together the orange juice, oil, vinegar, mustard, and honey. Season to taste with salt and pepper. Set aside.

4 Pat the salmon dry with paper towels and brush the non-skin side with a light coating of the dressing; season with salt and pepper.

5 Place a 10-inch skillet in the oven and heat for 5 minutes. Carefully remove the skillet from the oven and place the salmon skin side down in the skillet. Reduce the temperature to 275 degrees F. Roast the salmon until it flakes apart when gently pressed with your finger and is just opaque or reaches an internal

temperature of 135 degrees F (for medium-rare), 10 to 13 minutes, basting halfway through with additional dressing.

6   Remove the salmon from the skillet and transfer to plates. Add the black-eyed peas, pomegranate seeds, reserved orange segments, and ¼ cup dressing to the skillet over medium heat. Toss to warm through, about 3 minutes. Remove your skillet from the heat and carefully fold in the arugula and drizzle with additional dressing to taste. Serve the salad with the salmon.

TIP: If pomegranates aren't in season (because, let's face it, they rarely are), you can often find bags of just the seeds (arils) in the frozen aisle with the bags of other frozen fruits.

SKILLET MUSSEL MARINARA

This dish transports me to the ocean. It's briny but not salty, saucy but not swimming in liquid. Grab the freshest mussels you can find (see How to Pick Mussels on page 74) and use them quickly so things don't go from fresh to cesspool. The clam juice in the pasta may sound a bit strange, but it really helps to bring out the seafood flavors without being overwhelming. Fire-roasted tomatoes give the dish a campfire-esque flavor, while plenty of fresh basil keeps everything light and summery. Though you won't have the nice alliteration in your dish's name, you can make Clam Marinara if fresh mussels are not available.

MAKES 4 SERVINGS

1½ pounds mussels
2 tablespoons extra-virgin olive oil
1 small yellow onion, minced
4 medium cloves garlic, minced
1 anchovy fillet, rinsed and minced, or
    ½ teaspoon anchovy paste (optional)
1 teaspoon dried oregano
Pinch of red pepper flakes
1 (15-ounce) can crushed or diced fire-
    roasted tomatoes

1 (8-ounce) bottle clam juice
1 tablespoon balsamic vinegar
Kosher salt and freshly ground black
    pepper
2 cups chicken broth or water
8 ounces bucatini or spaghetti, broken
    into thirds
¼ cup chopped fresh basil
Crusty bread, for serving

1   Soak the mussels in a large bowl of cold water for 20 to 30 minutes to allow them to purge any grit. Drain and rinse, gently scrubbing, if needed. Debeard the mussels by pulling the clump of hairlike fibers poking out from the side of the mussel toward the hinge of the shell (some beards are harder to remove than others). Set aside.

2   Heat the oil in a 10-inch skillet over medium heat. Add the onions and cook until softened, about 5 minutes. Stir in the garlic, anchovy, oregano, and red pepper flakes and cook until fragrant, about 1 minute. Stir in the tomatoes and clam juice and gently simmer until the flavors are blended, about 5 minutes. Stir in the vinegar and season to taste with salt and pepper.

3   Add the broth to the skillet and bring to a boil. Carefully add the pasta, stirring gently until the pasta collapses and fits in your skillet. Cover and reduce to a simmer over medium-low heat. Cook, stirring often, until the pasta is just al dente, about 10 minutes. Add the mussels and continue to cook, covered, until the mussels have opened and the pasta is al dente, about 4 minutes.

4   Discard any unopened mussels. Scatter the basil over the noodles and serve with the crusty bread for dipping.

HOW TO PICK MUSSELS

Though mussels have a peak season (usually October through March), you can often find them year-round. You will want to buy them fresh and use them within a day or two, as they can go from delicious to dangerous in a short period of time. Look for mussels that are kept on ice, have a nice shiny shell that is tightly closed, and are not chipped. When you get home, unwrap your mussels, put them in a large bowl, cover them with a wet kitchen towel, and place them in the refrigerator. After cleaning the mussels (see the first step on page 73), discard any that have open shells that won't close up when gently pressed between your fingers—an open shell before cooking means the mussel has died and could greatly upset your tummy. Conversely, discard any mussels that are closed after cooking, because that means they are also no good to eat.

GINGER SHRIMP AND SUGAR SNAP PEAS

with Coconut Rice

Bright, colorful, and packed with flavor, this is one of those dishes that will become a regular visitor when you don't feel much like cooking. The ginger-laced shrimp and sugar snap peas lend enough protein and veg to the dish to be satisfying but still leave you with some get-up-and-go after the meal. The rice falls somewhere between a side dish and a dessert. It's definitely savory, with lime zest, green onions, and the pan juices from the shrimp. But that coconut . . . it's just sweet enough to keep you coming back for more, but not so much that you couldn't take another bite.

MAKES 4 SERVINGS

½ cup unsweetened coconut flakes
2 tablespoons sesame oil, divided
1 pound peeled and deveined shrimp
1 pound sugar snap peas, trimmed and cut in half on the diagonal
1 tablespoon minced peeled fresh ginger
3 medium cloves garlic, minced
2 tablespoons soy sauce
1 teaspoon sambal oelek (ground fresh chili paste; optional)

1 cup long-grain white rice, such as jasmine or basmati
1 (14-ounce) can unsweetened coconut milk
1 cup water
2 teaspoons fresh lime zest
3 green onions, light-green and white parts, thinly sliced
1 tablespoon freshly squeezed lime juice
Lime wedges, for serving

1 Heat a 10-inch skillet over medium-low heat. Add the coconut flakes to the dry skillet and toast until fragrant and golden, 1 to 2 minutes. Transfer the flakes from the skillet to a plate to cool.

2 Heat 1 tablespoon of the oil in your skillet over medium heat. Stir in the shrimp and snap peas and cook, stirring, until the shrimp are pink, 2 to 4 minutes. Add the ginger and garlic and cook until fragrant, about 1 minute. Toss with the soy sauce and sambal oelek, then transfer the shrimp mixture from the skillet to a bowl. Cover lightly with aluminum foil to keep warm.

3   Add the remaining 1 tablespoon oil to your skillet over medium heat. Stir in the rice and cook until the edges just begin to turn translucent, about 1 minute. Add the coconut milk, water, and lime zest and bring to a boil. Reduce the heat to a simmer and cook, covered, until the rice is tender and most of the liquid is absorbed, 10 to 12 minutes. Stir every once in a while so the rice doesn't stick to the bottom of your skillet.

4   When the rice is cooked, stir in the reserved toasted coconut flakes, green onions, and lime juice. Remove the skillet from the heat. Top the rice with the shrimp mixture, cover, and let steam for 5 minutes to warm through. Serve immediately with lime wedges for squeezing on the side.

SWAP IT OUT: If the snap peas at the grocery store look a little floppy, use 1 cup of parboiled shelled edamame.

CLAM AND BACON PIZZA

with Roasted Peppers, Kale, and Parmesan

This is not your traditional red sauce, pepperoni, and cheese pizza. Yes, there is sauce (balsamic vinegar and oil), yes, there is pig (bacon), and yes, there is cheese (Parmesan), so maybe consider this to be pizza with a twist. Since the two pizzas have to be cooked in batches (unless you own two cast iron skillets), you can make one and eat it while the other bakes, or pop the first back in the oven for a minute to warm up once the second is done. Usually, we chow down on the first, standing around the kitchen island, while the second is baking, then dig right in . . . again!

MAKES 4 SERVINGS

1 (1-pound) package store-bought pizza dough
6 slices bacon
1 large shallot, thinly sliced
2 medium cloves garlic, minced
1 small bunch lacinato kale (about 7 ounces), tough stems removed and leaves chopped
1 (10-ounce) can whole baby clams, drained and liquid reserved

1 tablespoon balsamic vinegar
Pinch of red pepper flakes
Kosher salt and freshly ground black pepper
Flour, for dusting
1 tablespoon extra-virgin olive oil, divided
½ cup jarred roasted peppers, drained and chopped, divided
1 cup (about 3 ounces) shredded Parmesan cheese, divided

1   Preheat the oven to 500 degrees F. Let the pizza dough rest at room temperature while the oven preheats.

2   Heat a 10-inch skillet over medium-low heat. Add the bacon and cook until just crisp, 6 to 8 minutes. Transfer to a paper-towel-lined plate until cool enough to handle. Chop the bacon and set aside.

3   Add the shallots to the fat in the pan and cook over medium-low heat until softened, about 3 minutes. Stir in the garlic and cook until fragrant, about 1 minute. Stir in the kale and ½ cup of the reserved clam liquid. Cook, covered, stirring occasionally, until the kale is tender, 5 to 7 minutes. Stir in the bacon, clams, vinegar, and red pepper flakes; season to taste with salt and pepper. Transfer the clam mixture to a plate. Wipe out the skillet with a paper towel.

4   Divide the pizza dough in half and roll it out on a lightly floured surface to fit your skillet. Add ½ tablespoon of the oil to the skillet and swirl to coat. Place the dough in the skillet and flip it over to lightly coat it with oil on both sides.

Sprinkle half of the clam mixture, half of the peppers, and half of the cheese over the dough.

5   Transfer the skillet to the oven and bake until the cheese is melted and the dough is cooked through, 8 to 12 minutes. Carefully remove the pizza to a cutting board and repeat with the remaining oil, dough, and toppings. Cut into wedges and serve.

TIP: Kale leaves can easily be removed from the ribs (stem) in two ways: You can lay the kale flat on a cutting board, with the rib end pointing toward you and, using a small knife, cut along the rib in a V shape. Or, and this is my favorite technique, hold the kale by the stem with one hand (with the leaf pointing down), grab around the base of the leaf with your other hand, and pull down in one firm sweep—the leaf will pull right off (and it's a fun way to get the kids involved in kitchen prep).

SMOKED SALMON FRITTATA

with Cream Cheese, Capers, and Dill

It's like your favorite delicatessen bagel, but in frittata form. All the essential ingredients are there—cream cheese, smoked salmon, onions, capers—minus the bagel. And, just like a good delicatessen bagel, you can eat it for breakfast, lunch, or dinner. If you really want the full experience, serve it alongside a bagel (of course, go for the "everything" or sesame bagel, not a cranberry-orange bagel—don't be a monster). Sometimes I even like to serve it with extra very thinly sliced red onions on the side, for a touch of brightness and crunch.

MAKES 4 TO 6 SERVINGS

8 large eggs
½ cup whole milk
2 tablespoons chopped fresh dill, or 2 teaspoons dried
Kosher salt and freshly ground black pepper
1 tablespoon extra-virgin olive oil
1 large red onion, thinly sliced

2 medium cloves garlic, minced
2 tablespoons capers, rinsed, drained, and roughly chopped
5 ounces baby spinach
½ pound smoked salmon, flaked
4 ounces cream cheese, cut into ½-inch cubes
Toasted bagels, for serving (optional)

1   Preheat the oven to 350 degrees F.
2   In a large bowl, whisk together the eggs, milk, and dill. Season to taste with salt and pepper.
3   Heat the oil in a 10-inch skillet over medium heat. Add the onions and cook until soft and golden, 10 to 12 minutes. Stir in the garlic and capers and cook until fragrant, 1 minute more. Add the spinach in handfuls and cook, stirring gently, until the spinach wilts, about 3 minutes. Fold in the salmon and season to taste with salt and pepper.
4   Pour the egg mixture over the salmon and stir to combine. Drop the cream cheese evenly over the top of the egg mixture. Cook over medium-low heat, without stirring, for 3 minutes.
5   Transfer the skillet to the oven and bake until the frittata is browned and puffed, 25 to 30 minutes. Let cool for 10 minutes before serving alongside the bagels.

TIP: What's the difference between smoked salmon and lox? Smoked salmon is cured in a brine, then smoked. Lox is simply cured, but not smoked. Smoked salmon has a heartier texture and tends to hold up better in a frittata, whereas lox has more of a "raw" texture and is great for layering in thin slices on bagels.

TUNA NOODLE SKILLET CASSEROLE

with Peas and Prosciutto

Best. Comfort. Food. Ever. And if that didn't convince you to try this creamy concoction of al dente noodles, tuna, cream, peas, and prosciutto, well . . . my father told me that when he was a medical resident, cough, many years ago, my very own grandmother used to make him tuna noodle casserole every Saturday for lunch. And, honest to God, he said my version was better. No disrespect, Grandma, but I got this! And you can get this too. I like to cook my noodles in chicken broth for extra flavor, but plain water will do the trick too. If you can't find prosciutto in the store, finely chop a few slices of bacon and cook until crisp.

MAKES 4 TO 6 SERVINGS

1 tablespoon extra-virgin olive oil
1 small yellow onion, diced
4 ounces prosciutto, diced
3 medium cloves garlic, minced
Kosher salt and freshly ground black pepper
Pinch of red pepper flakes (optional)
6 ounces (about 2 cups dry) orecchiette pasta

2 cups chicken broth
1½ cups half-and-half or heavy cream
1 (5.5-ounce) can water-packed albacore tuna, drained and flaked
1 cup frozen peas, thawed
1 cup (about 3 ounces) shredded Parmesan cheese, divided
½ cup panko bread crumbs

1 Heat the oil in a 10-inch skillet over medium heat. Add the onions and prosciutto and cook until the onions are softened, about 5 minutes. Stir in the garlic and cook until fragrant, about 1 minute. Season to taste with salt, pepper, and red pepper flakes.

2 Add the pasta to the skillet, then carefully stir in the broth and half-and-half. Bring to a gentle simmer, uncovered, and cook until the pasta is tender and the liquid has thickened, stirring often, 12 to 15 minutes.

3 Stir the tuna, peas, and half of the cheese into the pasta. Continue to cook, gently stirring, until heated through, about 3 minutes.

4 Preheat the broiler with the rack 6 inches from the element.

5 Sprinkle the bread crumbs and remaining cheese on top of the noodles. Transfer the skillet to the oven and broil until the cheese is melted and golden, 2 to 3 minutes. Let cool for 5 minutes before serving.

TOMATO-POACHED MAHI MAHI

with Zucchini and Fresh Herbs

Much like a good pair of pants, this dish is endlessly versatile. You can dress this up; you can dress it down. It always looks great, but it's also super cozy and easy to shimmy into (making, that is). Fresh fish fillets are gently poached in a tomato-based broth and then nestled lovingly among zucchini. The whole thing is finished with more fresh herbs than you can shake a stick at. Don't have or like mahi mahi? Simply swap it out with bass, cod, halibut, or salmon. Have a lot of summer squash growing in the garden this year? Here's a great way to use it up! Ditto with the herbs. Use any soft herbs you have on hand, but avoid the harder herbs (like rosemary and thyme) as they are not as palatable in texture or flavor.

MAKES 4 SERVINGS

4 (6-ounce) striped mahi mahi fillets, about 1 inch thick

Kosher salt and freshly ground black pepper

2 tablespoons extra-virgin olive oil

1 large onion, thinly sliced

2 medium zucchini (about 12 ounces), cut into ½-inch cubes

2 medium cloves garlic, minced

Pinch of red pepper flakes

1 (15-ounce) can diced tomatoes

½ cup vegetable or chicken broth

1 cup parsley, tarragon, basil, or chervil leaves, or a mixture, roughly chopped

1 tablespoon balsamic or sherry vinegar

Crusty bread, for serving

1   Pat the fish dry with paper towels and season with salt and pepper. Set aside.

2   Heat the oil in a 10-inch skillet over medium heat. Add the onions and cook until soft, about 5 minutes. Stir in the zucchini and cook until slightly softened, about 4 minutes. Add the garlic and red pepper flakes and cook until fragrant, about 1 minute. Season to taste with salt and pepper.

3   Pour in the tomatoes and broth and bring to a boil. Reduce to a simmer and let cook, covered, stirring occasionally, for 10 minutes to meld the flavors.

4   Gently place the fish in the sauce and adjust the heat to maintain a gentle simmer. Cook, covered, spooning the sauce over the fillets occasionally, until the fish flakes apart when gently pressed with your finger and is opaque, 5 to 7 minutes. If the fillets are not mostly submerged, turn them over halfway through.

5   Divide the fish between serving bowls. Mix the herbs and vinegar into the sauce in your skillet and season to taste with salt and pepper. Spoon the sauce over the fish and serve with the crusty bread for dipping.

TAKING FLIGHT:
Poultry Recipes

Let's play a bit of an off-brand game of "duck, duck, goose" and cast our net a little wider with "chicken, turkey, Cornish game hen." With a bit of duck thrown in for good measure. And to mix in yet another cliché: since birds of a feather flock together, you'll love playing around with these versatile recipes that range from simple (Turkey Pot Pie with a Twist, page 95) to fancy (Seared Duck Breasts with Fig and Arugula Salad, page 113) to everywhere in between.

Most of these recipes feature chicken. Why, you may ask? Chicken is safe, emotionally. Chicken is easy to find at every single grocery store, often inexpensive (or frequently on sale), familiar and tasty to most palates (I'm looking at you, kids and less-adventurous eaters . . . totally no judgment), and can be dressed up or down. It's also a good entry point to trying new recipes with flavors you may not normally use. Most of us have cooked a piece of chicken at some point in our lives, so there's little intimidation factor. Which means we're more willing to toss in some new flavors or try a different cooking technique. Of course, always handle chicken with care, washing your hands and work surfaces and making sure to cook it completely to the proper internal temperature so it's safe to consume as well. And just so we don't get stuck in a rut, you'll find a few other flocks from a feather mixed into this chapter, just for fun.

MISO CHICKEN

with Bok Choy and Mushrooms

Technically, this dish could make four servings, but it never quite stretches that far for us. The chicken, first crisped on the stove top, then cooked to perfection in the oven, has a sweet yet savory element that is difficult to stop eating. The bok choy and mushrooms cook just to al dente in the pan juices, giving them an extra layer of umami (savory) flavor. When picking bok choy, which is a type of Chinese cabbage, reach for the "baby" variety with bright-white stalks and nice green leaves. Remove about an inch of the base, separate the leaves, and rinse them under cool water before cooking. If you're portion-minded, and perhaps serving this with a side grain like cooked brown rice, it could easily serve four people. However, we are not those people. Pass me more miso chicken, please.

MAKES 2 TO 4 SERVINGS

4 bone-in, skin-on chicken thighs, trimmed

Kosher salt and freshly ground black pepper

¼ cup white or yellow miso paste

2 tablespoons rice vinegar

2 tablespoons honey

2 teaspoons minced peeled fresh ginger

2 teaspoons sesame oil

1 tablespoon high-heat oil, such as canola or safflower

8 baby bok choy (about 2 pounds), roots trimmed and leaves separated

8 ounces cremini or shiitake mushrooms, stemmed and thinly sliced

1   Preheat the oven to 425 degrees F.

2   Pat the chicken dry with paper towels and season with salt and pepper.

3   In a small bowl, whisk together the miso, vinegar, honey, ginger, and sesame oil. Set aside.

4   Heat the high-heat oil over medium heat in a 10-inch skillet. Add the chicken, skin side down, and cook until brown and crisp, 4 to 5 minutes. Turn and cook until the other side is brown, 2 to 3 minutes. Transfer the skillet to the oven and roast the chicken for 10 minutes.

5   Carefully remove the skillet from the oven and transfer the chicken to a plate. Drain off all but 1 tablespoon of the chicken fat from the skillet. Place the bok choy and mushrooms in the skillet and, using tongs, toss with 3 tablespoons of the miso mixture. Spread about 1 tablespoon of the miso mixture on top of each thigh and nestle the thighs on top of the bok choy. Return the skillet to the oven and continue to roast until the chicken reaches an internal temperature of 165 degrees F and the bok choy and mushrooms are tender, about 15 minutes.

→

6　Carefully remove the skillet from the oven and place the chicken thighs on serving plates. Gently toss the bok choy and mushrooms with the pan juices and serve alongside the chicken, basting with more pan juices as desired. Serve immediately.

TIP: It's salty, it's funky, it's sweet, it's earthy. Miso is a little bit of everything. At its core, miso is fermented soybeans inoculated with a mold called *koji*. It comes in a lighter, somewhat sweeter variety (white or yellow miso) and a darker, saltier version (red or brown). Though I suggest white or yellow miso for this recipe, red or brown would also be delicious if that's what you happen to have in your refrigerator.

CURRY POACHED CHICKEN AND COUSCOUS SALAD

Chicken is poached in an aromatic currified liquid (I know that's not a word, but it should be, amirite?) along with rainbow chard, then chopped up and mixed back in with couscous, sweet-tart currants, and crunchy cashews. I love that the couscous absorbs all of the flavors from the poaching liquid, making it especially flavorful. And it certainly doesn't hurt that the couscous only needs five minutes to cook once the chicken is done. I love to dollop plain Greek yogurt on top of the salad before serving, because yogurt makes everything better, in my opinion (and it adds nice creamy, fatty, and tart components to the dish).

MAKES 4 SERVINGS

2 (6-ounce) boneless, skinless chicken breasts, trimmed
Kosher salt and freshly ground black pepper
1 large bunch rainbow chard (about ½ pound)
2 tablespoons high-heat oil, such as canola or safflower, divided
1 small red onion, finely chopped

3 medium cloves garlic, minced
1 to 2 tablespoons yellow curry powder
1½ cups chicken stock
1 cup couscous
½ cup dried currants
½ cup roasted and salted cashews, roughly chopped
2 tablespoons chopped fresh cilantro
Plain Greek yogurt, for serving (optional)

1 Place the chicken between two sheets of parchment paper or plastic wrap and gently pound with a meat mallet or your cast iron skillet until it reaches an even thickness, about 1 inch thick. Pat the chicken dry with paper towels and season with salt and pepper.

2 Remove the leaves from the chard stems. Finely chop the stems and shred the leaves, keeping them separate.

3 Heat 1 tablespoon of the oil in a 10-inch skillet over medium heat. Add the chicken and cook until golden brown on both sides, flipping halfway through, 4 to 6 minutes. Transfer to a plate.

4 Add the remaining 1 tablespoon oil to your skillet over medium heat. Add the onions and chard stems and cook until softened, about 5 minutes. Add the chard leaves, a handful at a time, and cook until wilted. Stir in the garlic and curry powder to taste and cook until fragrant, about 1 minute. Season to taste with salt and pepper.

→

5 Pour in the chicken stock and nestle the chicken into the skillet. Bring to a simmer, cover, and reduce the heat to medium-low. Simmer the chicken until it reaches an internal temperature of 165 degrees F or the meat looks white throughout, about 10 minutes.

6 Transfer the chicken to a cutting board to cool, then chop into ¼-inch pieces.

7 Bring the chard-stock mixture back to a boil. Stir in the couscous and currants, cover, remove the skillet from the heat, and let stand for 5 minutes. Fluff the couscous with a fork, then fold in the chicken, cashews, and cilantro.

8 Portion the couscous onto four plates and dollop with the yogurt.

SWAP IT OUT: If you can't find dried currants, dried sweetened cranberries are a great substitute.

TURKEY POT PIE WITH A TWIST

Spoiler alert: the "twist" is that unlike traditional pot pies with an actual pie top, this version is topped with sliced baguettes. Why? First, because it's fun and easy. Second, because I usually always have a baguette around the kitchen. And third, I really don't like making pie crust. Along with cooked and shredded turkey, and the world's fastest bechamel sauce, this pot pie goes from stove top to dinner plate in about thirty minutes. I like to prepare all of my veggies ahead of time (sometimes the day before if I'm chopping other veggies for other meals), making this one of my quickest and easiest weeknight dinners. And don't toss that remaining baguette: use the first half as a topping and the second half for dipping.

MAKES 4 TO 6 SERVINGS

4 tablespoons unsalted butter
2 large carrots, diced
2 medium ribs celery, diced
1 small yellow onion, finely chopped
3 medium cloves garlic, minced
Kosher salt and freshly ground black
　pepper
4 tablespoons all-purpose flour
1½ cups chicken broth

1 cup whole milk or half-and-half
½ pound cooked and shredded turkey
1 cup frozen peas, thawed
16 to 20 (½-inch-thick) baguette slices
　(from about half a baguette)
Nonstick cooking spray
½ cup (about 1½ ounces) shredded
　Parmesan cheese

1　Melt the butter over medium heat in a 10-inch skillet. Add the carrots, celery, and onions and cook until the vegetables are soft, 5 to 7 minutes. Stir in the garlic and cook for 1 minute. Season to taste with salt and pepper.

2　Stir in the flour and cook for 1 minute. Slowly stir in the broth and milk, scraping up any browned spots and smoothing out the lumps. Bring to a simmer and cook for 5 minutes, stirring often.

3　Stir in the turkey and peas and continue to gently simmer, stirring often, until the sauce is thick and the flavors meld, about 5 minutes more. Season to taste with salt and pepper.

4　Preheat the broiler with the rack 8 inches from the element.

5　Lay the baguette slices on top of the filling, slightly overlapping. Lightly spray the bread with the oil, then sprinkle the cheese over the top. Broil until the cheese is melted and the bread is browned, about 2 minutes. Carefully remove the skillet from the oven and let cool for 5 minutes before serving.

SWAP IT OUT: You can easily substitute cooked and shredded chicken for the turkey.

EDAMAME-GINGER RICE

with Chicken

This is one of those easy weeknight dinners that everyone can enjoy. The rice is both colorful and flavorful, with spring-green edamame and zesty lime. The chicken is nonconfrontational, with just enough flavor from poaching in the ginger-scented rice to make it interesting but not overwhelming or intimidating. And the whole darn thing cooks together in about thirty minutes. This dish also has that strange quality of being simultaneously a bit out of the ordinary and also super comforting. Basically, it's magic: new, comforting, family-friendly, and pretty darn easy. Make sure you grab a bag of shelled edamame. If you use the ones still in the shell, you'll have a lot of messy work eating dinner!

MAKES 4 SERVINGS

1 pound boneless, skinless chicken breasts, trimmed

Kosher salt and freshly ground black pepper

2 tablespoons high-heat oil, such as canola or safflower, divided

1 small yellow onion, finely chopped

2 large carrots, cut into matchsticks

1 cup frozen shelled edamame

2 tablespoons minced peeled fresh ginger

4 medium cloves garlic, minced

1 teaspoon fresh lime zest

2¼ cups chicken broth

1 cup long-grain white rice, such as jasmine or basmati

2 tablespoons soy sauce

1 tablespoon sesame oil

1 tablespoon freshly squeezed lime juice

3 green onions, green and white parts thinly sliced

2 teaspoons toasted sesame seeds

1   Pat the chicken dry with paper towels and season with salt and pepper.

2   Heat 1 tablespoon of the high-heat oil in a 10-inch skillet over medium heat. Add the chicken and cook until golden brown on one side, 4 to 6 minutes. Transfer to a plate.

3   Add the remaining 1 tablespoon high-heat oil to the skillet. Add the onions and cook until soft, about 5 minutes. Stir in the carrots, edamame, ginger, garlic, and lime zest and cook until fragrant, about 1 minute. Season to taste with salt and pepper. Add the broth and rice and stir to combine.

4   Nestle the chicken, brown side up, in the rice and bring to a simmer. Reduce the heat to medium-low and cook, covered, until the chicken reaches an internal temperature of 165 degrees F, the liquid is absorbed, and the rice is tender, 15 to 17 minutes.

5   Remove the chicken from the rice and transfer to a cutting board. Remove the skillet from the heat and stir the soy sauce, sesame oil, lime juice, and green onions into the rice. Slice the chicken into ½-inch-thick slices and arrange on top of the rice. Sprinkle the dish with sesame seeds and serve.

ROASTED CHICKEN

with New Potatoes, Coriander, and Mint

On the surface, this is a pretty simple dish with just a few ingredients. But when you taste it, those simple ingredients combine together to make a surprisingly flavorful meal. Fresh mint and lemon zest are combined with aromatic coriander and garlic, then smothered all over the chicken and potatoes. The potatoes get even more flavor as they roast in the schmaltz (chicken fat) left after searing the chicken. There's a little legwork (pun intended—chicken thighs or drumsticks!) in the beginning, but then the whole kit and kaboodle does its thing in the oven for the majority of the cooking time.

MAKES 4 SERVINGS

4 bone-in, skin-on chicken thighs or drumsticks, trimmed
Kosher salt and freshly ground black pepper
4 tablespoons extra-virgin olive oil, divided
2 tablespoons chopped fresh mint

1 tablespoon ground coriander
3 medium cloves garlic, minced
2 teaspoons fresh lemon zest
1 pound new red or yellow potatoes, quartered
½ large red onion, thickly sliced
Lemon wedges, for serving

1   Preheat the oven to 450 degrees F with the rack positioned in the lower third of the oven.
2   Pat the chicken dry with paper towels and season liberally with salt and pepper. Set aside.
3   In a small bowl, combine 3 tablespoons of the oil with the mint, coriander, garlic, and lemon zest. Set aside.
4   Heat the remaining 1 tablespoon oil in a 10-inch skillet over medium heat. Add the chicken, skin side down, and cook until a deep golden brown, about 7 minutes. Flip the chicken and cook for 2 additional minutes. Transfer to a plate.
5   Add the potatoes and onions to the fat remaining in the skillet and toss to coat. Season with salt and pepper. Transfer the skillet to the oven and roast for 10 minutes.
6   Carefully remove the skillet from the oven and toss the potatoes with 2 tablespoons of the mint sauce. Nestle the chicken on top of the potatoes and schmear the top with the remaining mint sauce. Return the skillet to the oven and roast until the potatoes are tender and the chicken reaches an internal temperature of 165 degrees F or the meat looks white throughout, 30 to 40 minutes.
7   Carefully remove from the oven and let rest for 5 minutes before serving with the lemon wedges for squeezing.

TIP: New potatoes are simply baby potatoes before they get big. They have thin, delicate skins and won't fall apart (like mashed potatoes) when cut and cooked. You can also try fingerling or new purple potatoes in this recipe.

TURKEY SKILLET CHILI

with Cheddar Buttermilk Biscuits

Listen, I don't want to oversell this dish. But this is where the world's easiest chili meets the world's easiest biscuits for the world's greatest weeknight dinner. It comes together in a snap, using mostly pantry staples, but packs a ton of flavor. It's also a fairly healthy meal: ground turkey and plenty of veggies are the base of the chili. I like to use ground turkey that's a mix of white and dark meat because I find ground turkey breast to be a bit lackluster and dry. The biscuits pack a bit more punch with buttermilk, chives, and a ton of cheddar cheese. Life is all about balance, right? By the way, this one can be a bubbler, so I like to place my skillet on a large sheet pan before baking it in the oven.

MAKES 4 TO 6 SERVINGS

For the chili
2 tablespoons high-heat oil, such as canola or safflower
1 small yellow onion, chopped
1 medium red bell pepper, chopped
1 medium green bell pepper, chopped
1 pound ground turkey
3 medium cloves garlic, minced
2 tablespoons tomato paste
1 tablespoon chili powder
1 tablespoon dark brown sugar
1 teaspoon dried oregano
1 (15-ounce) can fire-roasted diced tomatoes

Kosher salt and freshly ground black pepper

For the biscuits
1 cup all-purpose flour
1 teaspoon baking powder
¼ teaspoon baking soda
¼ teaspoon kosher salt
3 tablespoons unsalted butter
1½ cups (6 ounces) shredded sharp cheddar cheese
⅔ cup buttermilk
2 tablespoons minced fresh chives

1   Preheat the oven to 425 degrees F.
2   To make the chili, heat the oil in a 10-inch skillet over medium heat. Add the onions and peppers and cook until tender, about 7 minutes. Add the ground turkey and cook until the meat is no longer pink, about 5 minutes. Stir in the garlic, tomato paste, chili powder, brown sugar, and oregano; cook until fragrant, about 1 minute. Add the tomatoes and stir to incorporate. Season to taste with salt and pepper. Remove from the heat.

→

3   To make the biscuits, in a large bowl, whisk together the flour, baking powder, baking soda, and salt. Cut the butter into the flour mixture with a pastry cutter or two forks until the mixture resembles coarse meal. Stir in the cheese, buttermilk, and chives and mix until just incorporated (the dough will be moist, like dumpling dough). Divide the batter into eight pieces and place on top of the chili.

4   Transfer the skillet to the oven and bake until the biscuits are golden brown, 20 to 25 minutes. Let cool for 10 minutes before serving.

TIP: If you don't have buttermilk on hand or don't feel like going to the store to buy a container, you can make your own. Combine ⅔ cup whole milk with a scant ½ tablespoon of white vinegar or lemon juice. Give it a stir and let it sit for 10 minutes to "sour" before using in the recipe.

GLAZED CHICKEN DRUMSTICKS

with Warm Carrot Salad

This was one of those recipes that started out as something completely different. Thanks to a few missing ingredients, a fight between the kiddos with building blocks, an unexpected visitor, and everything else that life likes to throw at us . . . it turned into an amazing meal. It was supposed to be much more complicated, but when push came to shove, all of the "salad" ingredients got tossed into the skillet with the chicken, everything was basted with the sweet-tangy-citrus sauce, and I couldn't be happier with the results. It's warm (both in flavors—thanks to orange, coriander, and cumin—and in temperature), savory (with those final touches of feta and mint), and packed with protein (hello, chicken and chickpeas). Dinner is served, no matter what happens to be going on!

MAKES 4 SERVINGS

4 tablespoons extra-virgin olive oil, divided

3 tablespoons freshly squeezed orange juice

3 tablespoons honey

3 tablespoons Dijon mustard

2 tablespoons apple cider vinegar

¾ teaspoon ground coriander

¾ teaspoon ground cumin

Kosher salt and freshly ground black pepper

Pinch of red pepper flakes

4 chicken drumsticks, trimmed

1 large shallot, thinly sliced

1 pound carrots, shredded

1 (15-ounce) can chickpeas, drained and rinsed

2 medium cloves garlic, minced

¼ cup dry white wine

1 cup (about 4 ounces) crumbled feta cheese

2 tablespoons chopped fresh mint

1   In a small bowl, whisk together 2 tablespoons of the oil, the orange juice, honey, mustard, vinegar, coriander, and cumin. Season to taste with salt, pepper, and red pepper flakes. Divide the dressing into three portions and set aside.

2   Preheat the oven to 400 degrees F.

3   Marinate the chicken in one-third of the dressing at room temperature for 30 minutes. Remove the chicken from the marinade and discard the marinade.

4   Heat 1 tablespoon of the oil in a 10-inch skillet over medium heat. Brown the chicken, 5 to 7 minutes, flipping halfway through. Remove the chicken from the skillet and drain off any fat.

5   Heat the remaining 1 tablespoon oil in your skillet over medium heat. Add the shallots and cook until softened, about 5 minutes. Stir in the carrots, chickpeas, and garlic and cook for 2 minutes. Deglaze the pan with the wine, scraping up any browned bits on the bottom.

→

6   Return the chicken to the skillet, nestling it on top of the carrot mixture. Transfer the skillet to the oven and cook until the chicken has reached an internal temperature of 165 degrees F or the meat looks white throughout, 25 to 35 minutes. Using another one-third of the marinade, baste the drumsticks every 5 to 10 minutes while roasting.

7   Carefully remove the skillet from the oven and transfer the chicken to a plate. Toss the carrot salad with the feta, mint, and remaining one-third dressing to taste. Serve the chicken alongside the warm carrot salad.

CHICKEN TAGINE

with Spiced Fennel Quinoa

Tagine is both a dish and a dish. It's a type of North African ceramic or clay dishware with a wide, shallow bowl and a distinctive domed top (the physical "dish"). It also refers to the meal made in such cookware, a slow-cooked stew-like meal, often with meat, vegetables, and fruit (the consumable "dish"). Though this version is not cooked in the traditional cookware (this is a skillet cookbook, after all), it does resemble the flavors: crisp chicken thighs, dried apricots, sweet and earthy fennel, chickpeas, and a ton of aromatic spices. If you're hungry, this is the meal for you, as my tagine is loaded with protein-packing chicken, quinoa, and beans.

MAKES 4 SERVINGS

2 tablespoons extra-virgin olive oil, divided
4 medium cloves garlic, minced
2 teaspoons fresh lemon zest
1 teaspoon minced fresh ginger
1 teaspoon smoked paprika
½ teaspoon ground cumin
½ teaspoon ground turmeric
½ teaspoon ground cinnamon
4 bone-in, skin-on chicken thighs, trimmed
Kosher salt and freshly ground black pepper

1 medium fennel bulb (about 8 ounces), trimmed, cored, and thinly sliced
1 (15-ounce) can chickpeas, rinsed and drained
½ cup dry white wine
1½ cups chicken broth
½ cup pitted Castelvetrano olives, halved
½ cup dried apricots, halved
½ cup quinoa, rinsed and drained
3 green onions, white and green parts chopped

1   Preheat the oven to 350 degrees F.
2   In a small bowl, combine 1 tablespoon of the oil with the garlic, lemon zest, ginger, paprika, cumin, turmeric, and cinnamon; set aside.
3   Pat the chicken dry with paper towels and season with salt and pepper. Heat the remaining 1 tablespoon oil in a 10-inch skillet over medium heat. Cook the

chicken, skin side down, until the skin is brown and crisp, 8 to 10 minutes. Flip the chicken and cook for 1 additional minute. Transfer to a plate, skin side up.

4   Pour off all but 2 tablespoons of fat from the skillet and add the fennel. Cook, stirring occasionally, until lightly browned, 5 to 7 minutes. Push the fennel to the side of the skillet. Add the reserved spice mixture and cook for 15 seconds. Stir in the fennel, add the chickpeas, and stir to coat. Add the wine and cook until almost evaporated, 1 to 2 minutes.

5   Add the broth, olives, and apricots to the skillet; bring to a boil. Stir in the quinoa and nestle the chicken, skin side up, in the skillet. Remove from the heat, cover the skillet with a lid, and transfer it to the oven. Roast until the chicken reaches an internal temperature of 165 degrees F and the quinoa is cooked through, 30 to 35 minutes. Sprinkle with the green onions before serving.

EASY CHICKEN ENCHILADA SKILLET

This one is a bit of a hot mess, but in a really good creamy, warm, and filling kind of way. Leftover chicken is given new life with spices, pinto beans, and fresh cilantro and then simmered in salsa and sour cream. Corn tortillas are mixed into the lot (no messy rolling of enchiladas here, so not entirely a hot mess after all!), then it's all topped with cheese. It also happens to be kid-approved, especially if you opt for milder and sweeter salsa. Or you can up your game for the sports-watching gang and go for the spicy stuff.

MAKES 4 TO 6 SERVINGS

2 tablespoons high-heat oil, such as canola or safflower
1 small yellow onion, chopped
3 medium cloves garlic, minced
1 teaspoon ground cumin
1 teaspoon ground coriander
1 teaspoon dried oregano
2 cups shredded cooked chicken
1 (15-ounce) can pinto beans, drained and rinsed

Kosher salt and freshly ground black pepper
1 (16-ounce) jar mild to spicy red salsa
1 cup chicken broth or water
½ cup sour cream
3 tablespoons chopped fresh cilantro
6 (6-inch) corn tortillas, cut into eighths
1 cup (about 4 ounces) shredded Mexican blend cheese
Lime wedges, for serving

1 Heat the oil in a 10-inch skillet over medium heat. Add the onions and cook until softened, about 5 minutes. Stir in the garlic, cumin, coriander, and oregano and cook until fragrant, about 1 minute. Add the chicken and beans. Season to taste with salt and pepper.

2 Pour in the salsa and broth and bring to a simmer. Cook at a gentle simmer, stirring occasionally, to warm the chicken through and meld the flavors, about 10 minutes. Fold in the sour cream and cilantro. Carefully stir in the tortillas, a handful at a time, until they are coated with the sauce and submerged in the skillet. Sprinkle the cheese over the top.

3 Preheat the broiler to high heat with the rack 6 inches from the element.

4 Transfer the skillet to the oven and broil until the cheese is melted and bubbling, 3 to 4 minutes. Serve with the lime wedges for squeezing.

TIP: If you leave the tortillas out of the dish and serve it with tortilla chips, it makes an awesome dip for a crowd.

ROASTED CHICKEN
with Braised White Beans and Bacon

I can't exactly pinpoint why, but this dish always reminds me of home. As in the Pacific Northwest "home," not necessarily my childhood house (because my mom never cooked bacon, see page 159). Maybe because it's classic comfort food for a cool evening. Perfect for those drizzly gray days when you need something hearty and warming. Chicken is slowly braised with crispy bacon, creamy white beans, and aromatics (onions, carrots, celery, and rosemary), making it creamy, smoky, and herbal. Bonus points: it's also fairly easy to put together for a relatively hands-off weeknight meal.

MAKES 4 SERVINGS

4 bone-in, skin-on chicken thighs or drumsticks, trimmed
Kosher salt and freshly ground black pepper
1 tablespoon high-heat oil, such as canola or safflower
6 slices bacon, chopped
1 small yellow onion, chopped
2 medium ribs celery, chopped

2 medium carrots, chopped
3 medium cloves garlic, minced
1 tablespoon chopped fresh rosemary, or 1 teaspoon dried
Pinch of red pepper flakes
1 (15-ounce) can cannellini or great northern beans, rinsed and drained
1 cup chicken broth

1   Preheat the oven to 425 degrees F.
2   Pat the chicken dry with paper towels and season with salt and pepper.
3   Heat the oil in a 10-inch skillet over medium heat. Cook the chicken, skin side down, until a deep golden brown, about 7 minutes. Flip the chicken and cook for 2 additional minutes. Transfer the chicken to a plate and drain the fat from the skillet.
4   Add the bacon to the skillet and cook over medium-low heat until it just starts to crisp, about 5 minutes. Stir in the onions, celery, and carrots and cook until softened, stirring often, about 7 minutes. Stir in the garlic, rosemary, and red pepper flakes and cook until fragrant, about 1 minute. Season to taste with salt and pepper.
5   Add the beans and broth to the skillet and stir to combine. Return the chicken to the skillet and nestle it in the beans, skin side up. Transfer the skillet to the oven and roast until the chicken reaches an internal temperature of 165 degrees F or the meat looks white throughout, 30 to 40 minutes. Let cool for 5 minutes before serving.

SEARED DUCK BREASTS

with Fig and Arugula Salad

Life is about balance. It can be rich (duck), salty (blue cheese), sweet (figs), spicy (arugula), crunchy (hazelnuts), even tangy (balsamic vinegar). Oh heck, I just described this salad! Despite what you may think, duck is easy to prepare. It basically cooks in its own (super-delicious) fat. When preparing the duck, the deeper you cut the fat, the more fat it will cook off, but be careful not to cut all the way through the skin to the flesh. It's easiest to cut the fat when the duck is still cold. Speaking of fat, do not throw the fat left over in your skillet down the drain. Save it in a small container in the fridge, and use it instead of oil or butter in any of the recipes in this book that call for potatoes.

MAKES 4 SERVINGS

4 medium duck breasts (about 1½ pounds)
Kosher salt and freshly ground black
  pepper
2 tablespoons extra-virgin olive oil
16 dried figs, stemmed and quartered
1 large shallot, halved and thinly sliced
1 teaspoon five-spice powder

¼ cup freshly squeezed orange juice (from
  1 large orange)
3 tablespoons balsamic vinegar
1 tablespoon honey
5 ounces baby arugula
½ cup crumbled blue cheese
¼ cup hazelnuts, toasted and chopped

1   With a sharp knife, score the duck breast skin in a crosshatch pattern, about ⅛ inch apart. Season the duck with salt and pepper.

2   Place the duck breasts, skin side down, in a cold (yes, cold!) 10-inch skillet. Heat the skillet over medium-low heat. Cook, without moving the duck breasts, until most of the fat has rendered, the skin is golden brown, and it reaches an internal temperature of 125 degrees F, about 15 minutes. Pour off the rendered fat as it cooks.

3   Increase the heat to medium and flip the breasts over. Cook until the duck reaches your desired doneness: 1 to 2 minutes for medium-rare (135 degrees F), 2 to 4 minutes for medium (140 degrees F), or 4 to 6 minutes for well done (155 degrees F). Remove the duck from the skillet and transfer to a cutting board; let it cool slightly. Thinly slice the duck and set aside. Drain the fat from the skillet (keep it for cooking!).

4   Heat the oil in the empty skillet over medium heat. Add the figs and shallots and cook until softened, about 3 minutes. Stir in the five-spice powder and cook until fragrant, about 30 seconds. Remove the skillet from the heat and stir in the orange juice, vinegar, and honey; season to taste with salt and pepper. Fold in the sliced duck.

5   In a large serving bowl, toss the duck mixture with the arugula. Sprinkle with the blue cheese and hazelnuts; serve immediately.

SWAP IT OUT: Swap out the dried figs with the real fresh thing. Stem and quarter about 12 fresh figs and toss them with the sliced duck at the end of cooking to heat through.

ORANGE-TARRAGON CORNISH GAME HENS

with Roasted Beets and Pistachios

Some folks are skeptical of beets. I will admit, they are earthy, they are rooty, and they can stain the heck out of your hands. But when prepared correctly, they are also sweet, tender, and, well . . . earthy. You can use red, yellow, Chioggia (those fun pink-striped ones), or a combination. Paired with fresh orange, crunchy pistachios, and the drippings from the cutest little hens you ever laid your eyes on, the beets in this dish may just change your opinion. Something important to consider when preparing this recipe is your appetite. If you're a dainty or moderate eater, this dish can easily serve four (each sharing a hen; simply cut it in half with a large knife or kitchen shears after it's cooked). If you're my husband or nephew, it makes a perfect meal for two.

MAKES 2 TO 4 SERVINGS

1 large Cara Cara or navel orange
3 tablespoons unsalted butter, melted
1 tablespoon chopped fresh tarragon, divided
1 teaspoon honey
Pinch of red pepper flakes
4 medium shallots, thickly sliced

2 large beets (about 1 pound), any color, peeled and cut into 1-inch chunks
1 tablespoon extra-virgin olive oil
Kosher salt and freshly ground black pepper
2 (1½-pound) Cornish game hens
¼ cup toasted pistachios

1 Preheat the oven to 400 degrees F with the rack at the lowest position.
2 Grate 2 teaspoons of zest from the orange and set aside. Remove the peel and pith and cut the orange into segments, then cut the segments into 1-inch pieces; set aside.
3 In a small bowl, combine the butter, orange zest, half of the tarragon, honey, and red pepper flakes. Set aside.
4 Toss the shallots and beets in a 10-inch skillet with the oil and season to taste with salt and pepper. Place the hens, breast side up, in your skillet, nestled on top of the vegetables. Season the hens liberally with salt and pepper and baste with some of the butter mixture.
5 Transfer the skillet to the oven and roast until the hens reach an internal temperature of 165 degrees F and the beets are tender, 60 to 70 minutes. Baste with the butter mixture every 15 minutes. Transfer the hens to a plate and let stand for 10 minutes before serving. Meanwhile, toss the beet mixture with the pan juices, pistachios, reserved orange segments, and remaining tarragon. Serve the hens over the beet mixture.

TIP: Can't find game hens at your grocery store? Check out the freezer section . . . they usually hide them there.

PARMESAN CHICKEN TENDERS

with Warm Fennel, Apple, and Arugula Salad

We call this one the "compromise meal." The kids are stoked to get crispy chicken fingers with sliced apples. The parents are equally stoked to get Parmesan-crusted chicken tenders with caramelized fennel, tossed with arugula and vinaigrette. It's a win-win. Don't want to buy chicken tenders? You can cut about 1½ pounds of chicken breasts into strips and call it a day. It may require a little more time and effort on your part, but it will also save you a few bucks. To keep things a bit tidier, whenever I'm doing a dredged cutlet (chicken, pork, or fish), I like to designate an egg hand and a bread crumb hand. This keeps things somewhat cleaner and easier to manage, and you don't end up with a hand covered in breading.

MAKES 4 SERVINGS

2 tablespoons apple cider vinegar
1 tablespoon Dijon mustard
1 tablespoon honey
3 tablespoons plus 1 teaspoon extra-virgin olive oil, divided
Kosher salt and freshly ground black pepper
1 medium fennel bulb (about 8 ounces), trimmed, cored, and very thinly sliced
1 large sweet-tart apple, like Fuji or Gala, halved, cored, and very thinly sliced

2 large eggs
2 tablespoons whole milk
2 cups panko bread crumbs
2 cups (about 6 ounces) shredded Parmesan cheese
1½ pounds (about 16) chicken tenders
¾ to 1 cup high-heat oil, such as canola or safflower, for frying, as needed
5 ounces baby arugula

1 In a small bowl, whisk together the vinegar, mustard, and honey. While whisking constantly, drizzle in 3 tablespoons of the olive oil to create an emulsified vinaigrette. Season to taste with salt and pepper and set aside.

2 Heat the remaining 1 teaspoon olive oil in a 10-inch skillet over medium heat. Add the fennel and cook until just barely softened, 2 to 4 minutes. Remove from the heat and toss with the apples and half the vinaigrette. Transfer to a bowl and cover to keep warm.

3   In a shallow dish, beat the eggs and milk together. Season to taste with salt and pepper. Combine the panko and cheese in another shallow dish. Working with one tender at a time, dredge in the egg mixture, allowing the excess to drip off, then coat all sides in the panko mixture, pressing gently to adhere. Move the chicken to a plate.

4   Heat a generous ¼ cup high-heat oil and a pinch of panko in your skillet over medium heat. When the panko turns golden brown, add one-third of the chicken tenders to the skillet. Cook, without moving, until the bottoms are a deep golden brown, 2 to 3 minutes. Using tongs, carefully flip the tenders over and cook until golden brown, 2 to 3 minutes more. Transfer the tenders to a paper-towel-lined baking sheet and season to taste with salt and pepper. Pour out any remaining oil. Repeat with the remaining oil and tenders.

5   Toss the arugula with the reserved fennel salad. Drizzle the chicken tenders with the remaining vinaigrette. Serve the salad with the chicken tenders.

TIP: Waste not, want not. If your fennel comes with the stalks and fronds still attached, thinly slice the stalks and toss them in with the sliced bulb when cooking. Chop the fronds and toss them in the final salad along with the arugula.

CHICKEN THIGHS

with Broccolini, Lemon, and Israeli Couscous

Familiar flavors with a bit of color and acid make this an easy, delicious, and, dare I say, entertaining weeknight meal. It may seem funny to add whole lemon slices, rind and all, to the skillet, but doing so adds a really rich and deep lemon flavor that's more than just a smidgen of zest. And if you're at all confused (like my hubby): do not eat the lemon slices after they are cooked, just push them off to the side as you're eating. If you can't find broccolini—baby broccoli with small florets and long slender stems (not to be confused with broccoli rabe, which has a stronger, more bitter flavor)—you can use asparagus for an equally yummy meal.

MAKES 4 SERVINGS

4 bone-in, skin-on chicken thighs, trimmed
Kosher salt and freshly ground black pepper
1 tablespoon high-heat oil, such as canola or safflower
1 tablespoon unsalted butter
1 small lemon, ends discarded, thinly sliced with seeds removed

1 cup Israeli (pearl) couscous
3 medium cloves garlic, minced
½ cup dry white wine
1¾ cups chicken broth
12 ounces broccolini (baby broccoli), cut into 1-inch pieces
½ cup (about 4 ounces) crumbled feta cheese
¼ cup fresh basil leaves, sliced

1 Pat the chicken thighs dry with paper towels and season with salt and pepper.
2 Heat the oil in a 10-inch skillet over medium heat. Add the chicken and cook, skin side down, until golden brown, about 7 minutes. Flip and cook on the other side, 5 minutes more. Transfer the chicken to a plate and set aside. Drain any fat from the skillet.
3 Add the butter and lemon slices to your skillet over medium heat. Cook until the lemons release their juices and start to brown, about 1 minute. Transfer to the plate with the chicken.
4 Add the couscous and garlic to your skillet; stir to coat with the fat in the pan and cook for 1 minute. Deglaze (scrape up any browned bits with a wooden spoon) the skillet with the wine and cook until the liquid is almost completely absorbed, about 1 minute.

5   Add the broth and lemon slices to your skillet and bring to a boil. Nestle the chicken, skin side up, into the couscous and place the broccolini around the chicken. Cover the skillet and reduce to a simmer over low heat. Cook until the couscous is tender and the chicken reaches an internal temperature of 165 degrees, 10 to 12 minutes.

6   Transfer the chicken to serving plates. Sprinkle the feta and basil over the couscous, season to taste with salt and pepper, and serve alongside the chicken.

TIP: Israeli couscous is the larger, chewier cousin of "regular" couscous. While both are made of semolina flour, Israeli couscous takes 10 to 12 minutes to cook (much like pasta), compared to the regular stuff that absorbs hot water and is ready in about 5 minutes. Though related, the two types of couscous are not interchangeable in this recipe, so buyer beware!

DIJON-ROASTED CHICKEN
with Italian Sausage and Brussels Sprouts

Is there anything better than brussels sprouts? (Now would be a good time to admit that I'm obsessed.) How about chicken thighs smothered in a sweet and savory honey-mustard sauce? (I also must admit that I'm a bit obsessed with mustard.) How can we top that? Sprinkle the whole darn thing with sausage! This is one of those meals when you want it all: poultry, vegetables, and pork. And, except for a little bit of prep beforehand, the whole thing is relatively hands-off. Because there is a bit of fat from both the olive oil and sausage, make sure to trim your chicken thighs really well, taking off any extra skin and fat that is hanging away from the meat so the overall dish isn't too oily.

MAKES 4 SERVINGS

3 tablespoons Dijon mustard
2 tablespoons honey
2 tablespoons extra-virgin olive oil, divided
1 tablespoon Worcestershire sauce
3 medium cloves garlic, minced
1 pound brussels sprouts, trimmed and halved if small or quartered if large

4 medium shallots, quartered
Kosher salt and freshly ground black pepper
4 bone-in, skin-on chicken thighs, trimmed
2 large sweet Italian sausages, cut into 1-inch pieces

1 Preheat the oven to 450 degrees F with the rack positioned in the lower third of the oven.
2 In a small bowl, combine the mustard, honey, 1 tablespoon of the oil, Worcestershire, and garlic. Set aside.
3 In a 10-inch skillet, toss the brussels sprouts and shallots with 2 tablespoons of the mustard sauce and the remaining 1 tablespoon oil. Season to taste with salt and pepper.
4 Pat the chicken dry with paper towels and season with salt and pepper. Nestle the chicken and sausage pieces on top of the brussels sprouts and pour the remaining mustard sauce over the chicken.
5 Roast in the oven until the brussels sprouts are browned and tender and the chicken reaches an internal temperature of 165 degrees F, 35 to 40 minutes. Carefully remove the skillet from the oven and let cool for 5 minutes before serving.

COWABUNGA:

Beef Recipes

This is what is often happening around here for dinner. Why, you may ask? First and foremost, my husband is a big fan of beef and requests a nice steak for dinner more often than not. Second, beef is endlessly versatile. And third . . . I just happen to have a quarter of a cow in my garage chest freezer, so we eat a lot of it because, frankly, we have a lot of it.

Beef can be ground, it can be cubed, it can be sliced, and it can be left just how it is in a perfect steak form. And each cut has its own distinctive texture and flavor. Whether you're cooking up a traditional patty melt (see Classic Patty Melts with Caramelized Onions and Cheddar, page 143), preparing a not-so-traditional kawarma (see Spiced Beef and Chickpea–Stuffed Pitas "Kawarma," page 155), smothering a steak in blue cheese (see Herb-Crusted Flank Steak with Sauteed Grapes and Blue Cheese, page 139), or turning it into curry (see Beef, Green Bean, and Pineapple Red Curry, page 147), you really can't go wrong. These recipes run the gauntlet from traditional and comforting to new and boundary-pushing. You'll find something your kids will like, you'll find something your guests will like, and, gosh darn it, you'll definitely find something that you will like.

STIR-FRIED TERIYAKI BEEF
with Broccoli

I would like to tell you that the ingenious crunchy ramen topping in this recipe was born because I am a one-skillet, one-meal master. Truth be told, teriyaki beef with broccoli is a staple at our house. It's easy to make and the kids love the salty-sweet sauce, so much so that they will even attempt a few bites of broccoli. However, I normally serve it with yakisoba noodles. Well, one hangry evening I realized that I forgot to buy yakisoba and it was too late to make a pot of rice, so . . . I crumbled some of their much-loved ramen noodles on top, totally uncooked, and handed them their plates. Instant winner and moment of *genius*. It's easiest to cut the flank steak super thin when the steak has been placed in the freezer for about thirty minutes.

MAKES 4 SERVINGS

1 pound flank steak
6 tablespoons soy sauce, divided
2 tablespoons plus 1 teaspoon white sugar, divided
½ cup chicken broth
2 tablespoons mirin or white wine
2 teaspoons cornstarch
Pinch of red pepper flakes (optional)
2 tablespoons plus 1 teaspoon sesame oil, divided

2 medium shallots, thickly sliced
1 medium head broccoli (about 1 pound), cut into small florets
½ cup water
3 medium cloves garlic, minced
1 tablespoon minced peeled fresh ginger
2 (3-ounce) packets ramen noodles, flavor packets discarded

1 Trim the flank steak of excess fat. Cut it into 2-inch-wide strips with the grain, then into ⅛-inch-thick slices against the grain. In a medium bowl, toss the beef with 3 tablespoons of the soy sauce and 1 teaspoon of the sugar. Let rest for 10 minutes.

2 In a separate bowl, whisk together the remaining 3 tablespoons soy sauce, remaining 2 tablespoons sugar, broth, mirin, cornstarch, and red pepper flakes. Set aside.

3 Heat 1 tablespoon of the oil in a 10-inch skillet over medium-high heat. Add half the beef in a single layer and cook, without stirring, for 1 minute. Stir the beef and cook until browned, an additional 1 to 2 minutes. Transfer the beef and any pan juices to a plate. Repeat with the remaining beef.

4 Add 1 tablespoon of the oil to your skillet over medium heat. Add the shallots and cook until just starting to soften, about 3 minutes. Add the broccoli and cook, stirring often, for an additional 2 minutes. Add the water and cook, covered, until the broccoli is just tender, 3 to 4 minutes.

5   Uncover the skillet and push the vegetables to one side. Add the remaining 1 teaspoon oil, garlic, and ginger to the center of your skillet. Cook until fragrant, about 30 seconds. Stir the garlic-ginger mixture into the broccoli. Stir in the beef, along with any juices.

6   Whisk the sauce mixture to recombine and pour over the beef and broccoli. Cook, tossing constantly, until the sauce has thickened, 1 to 2 minutes. Crumble the ramen over the beef and broccoli mixture, stir gently to combine, and serve immediately.

TIP: If you like a slightly softer ramen (more noodle-like), stir it into the beef mixture, cover the skillet, and let it sit for 5 minutes before serving.

SKILLET INSIDE-OUT TACO BAKE

The kids refer to this one as an "inside-out taco." All the good things you expect from a taco: a not-too-spicy-with-a-hint-of-sweet meat filling, refried beans, tomatoes, cheese, and, of course, crunchy tortillas. But it's just all in the wrong order. And it's really more like a luscious, gooey casserole dip. Instead of trying to stuff all of this goodness inside of the shell (because, let's face it . . . that never works out well), it's just layered in a skillet. It's easier to eat (which means you get to eat more of it, right?), tastes just as awesome, and (most likely) won't leave a giant stain down the front of your shirt. If you really want to up your taco game, serve this dish with some shredded lettuce and sour cream.

MAKES 4 TO 6 SERVINGS

1 tablespoon high-heat oil, such as canola or safflower

1 small yellow onion, finely chopped

1 pound lean ground beef

4 medium cloves garlic, minced

1 tablespoon chili powder

1 tablespoon packed dark brown sugar

2 teaspoons apple cider vinegar

½ teaspoon dried oregano

2 (10-ounce) cans diced tomatoes with green chilies (mild or hot), drained and divided

Kosher salt and freshly ground black pepper

1 (15-ounce) can refried beans

2 cups (about 4 ounces) broken tortilla chips, divided, plus additional whole chips, for serving

2 cups (about 8 ounces) shredded Mexican blend cheese, divided

¼ cup chopped fresh cilantro

Lime wedges, for serving

1   Preheat the oven to 375 degrees F.
2   Heat the oil in a 10-inch skillet over medium heat. Add the onions and cook until tender, about 5 minutes. Add the beef, breaking it into small pieces with a wooden spoon, and cook until browned, 5 to 7 minutes. Stir in the garlic, chili powder, brown sugar, vinegar, oregano, and half of the tomatoes; cook for 1 minute. Season to taste with salt and pepper.
3   In a small bowl, combine the remaining tomatoes and the beans.
4   Spread the beef in a flat layer on the bottom of the skillet. Sprinkle with half of the chips and half of the cheese. Dollop and then spread the bean mixture over the top. Top with the remaining chips and cheese.
5   Bake until the filling is warm and the cheese is golden, about 20 minutes. Carefully remove from the oven and let cool for 10 minutes before serving. Sprinkle with the cilantro and serve with the lime wedges for squeezing and additional tortilla chips for dipping.

MEATBALLS

with Caramelized Onions and Pine Nut Lemon Rice

This dish falls under "ultimate comfort food." It's got enough things going on (sweet-savory caramelized onions, lemon, crunchy pine nuts) to keep it interesting, but doesn't go too deep into uncharted territory (meatballs and rice). The beauty of this meal is that the meatballs and rice cook together in the same pot, at the same time, infusing both with flavor. It's warm, it's filling, it's filled with meat and carbs, it will keep you safe and let you know that you are loved. You can prepare the meatballs a day or two ahead of time and keep them refrigerated until you're ready to fry them in your skillet, to cut down a little on the weeknight dinner madness.

MAKES 4 SERVINGS

1 pound lean ground beef
1 medium yellow onion, finely chopped, divided
¼ cup chopped fresh parsley, divided
3 tablespoons dried bread crumbs
1 large egg
1 tablespoon fresh lemon zest, divided
Kosher salt and freshly ground black pepper
2 tablespoons extra-virgin olive oil

3 medium cloves garlic, minced
1 cup long-grain white rice, such as jasmine or basmati
2 cups chicken broth
2 tablespoons freshly squeezed lemon juice
¼ cup (about ¾ ounce) shredded Parmesan cheese
¼ cup toasted pine nuts

1   In a large bowl, combine the beef, ¼ cup of the minced onions, 2 tablespoons of the parsley, bread crumbs, egg, and 1½ teaspoons of the lemon zest. Season to taste with salt and pepper. Mix with your hands until thoroughly combined.

2   Divide the mixture into 16 balls. Refrigerate for at least 15 minutes or up to 24 hours.

3   Heat the oil in a 10-inch skillet over medium heat. Cook the meatballs until well browned, turning occasionally, 5 to 7 minutes. Transfer the meatballs to a plate.

4   Add the remaining onions to the fat left in the skillet. Cook over medium-low heat, stirring occasionally, until a deep golden brown, 10 to 15 minutes. Stir in the garlic and cook until fragrant, about 1 minute. Add the rice and stir until the edges begin to turn translucent, about 1 minute. Season to taste with salt and pepper. Stir in the broth, lemon juice, and remaining lemon zest. Bring to a boil.

5   Return the meatballs to the skillet, cover, and reduce to a simmer. Cook until the rice is tender and the meatballs are cooked through, about 20 minutes. Remove from the heat and let sit, covered, for 5 minutes. Sprinkle with the Parmesan, pine nuts, and remaining parsley before serving.

STEAK TIPS AND CAULIFLOWER "CAPONATA" SALAD

Caponata is an Italian dish usually made with eggplant, capers, and an *agrodolce* (sweet and sour) sauce. And that was what this dish was supposed to be, until I forgot to buy the darn eggplant at the store. However, I did have a head of cauliflower lingering in the fridge, and as all good discoveries go . . . necessity is the mother of invention. So here we have a twist on the traditional caponata, where cauliflower is cooked until golden brown in the skillet, then tossed with sweet roasted peppers, salty capers, and fresh parsley. The whole kit and kaboodle is topped with medium-rare steak bites crusted in herbs for a salad like no other. Because I'm a fan of anything with cheese on top, this dish has a healthy serving of shredded Gruyère cheese sprinkled over it. If dairy isn't your thing, omit it from the recipe (don't worry: it's still going to be delicious).

MAKES 4 SERVINGS

1 cup jarred roasted red bell peppers, drained and chopped

5 tablespoons extra-virgin olive oil, divided

2 tablespoons chopped fresh parsley

2 tablespoons capers, rinsed, drained, and chopped

1 large head cauliflower (about 2 pounds), cored and cut into 1-inch florets

3 medium cloves garlic, minced

Kosher salt and freshly ground black pepper

2 teaspoons onion powder

1 teaspoon garlic powder

1 teaspoon dried oregano

½ teaspoon smoked paprika

2 pounds sirloin steak tips, trimmed and cut into 2-inch pieces

1 cup (about 2½ ounces) shredded Gruyère cheese

1   Combine the peppers, 1 tablespoon of the oil, parsley, and capers in a large bowl. Set aside.

2   Heat 2 tablespoons of the oil in a 10-inch skillet over medium heat. Add the cauliflower and cook, covered, stirring occasionally, until browned and tender, 12 to 15 minutes. Stir in the garlic and cook for 1 additional minute. Season to taste with salt and pepper. Add the cauliflower to the pepper mixture and

toss to combine. Set aside in the bowl or on a serving platter, covered with aluminum foil to keep warm.

3   Combine the onion powder, garlic powder, oregano, and paprika in another large bowl. Toss the steak tips in the seasoning. Transfer them to a plate, shaking off any extra seasoning. Season the steak tips with salt and pepper.

4   Heat the remaining 2 tablespoons oil in your skillet over medium heat. Add the steak tips and cook until golden brown on all sides and it reaches an internal temperature of 135 degrees F (for medium-rare), 6 to 10 minutes, stirring gently on occasion.

5   Divide the cauliflower mixture between four plates and top with the steak tips. Sprinkle with the cheese and serve immediately.

SWAP IT OUT: Instead of sirloin steak tips, you can also use beef tenderloin or flank steak. Just don't use stew meat—while it may look the same (size and shape), it will be much too tough for this salad.

CHEESEBURGER MACARONI

Kids are brutally honest, and mine have nicknamed this dish "ugly pasta." I'm not going to argue with them—this isn't the prettiest meal in my repertoire, but it is one of the family favorites. Without stepping on any copyright toes, I'll say it's basically a homemade, high-class Hamburger Helper. It's super savory, thanks to bacon and ground beef, has a touch of spice (think flavor, not hot . . . totally kid-approved) from smoked paprika, and ends on a high note of everyone's favorite pasta shape (macaroni) immersed in creamy, cheesy goodness. And it makes a lot, so it is perfect for a crowd or fantastic for lunch leftovers. You can also freeze it in individual portions for quick microwave-ready meals to reheat on the go when you need a fast lunch or dinner.

MAKES 6 SERVINGS

1½ tablespoons high-heat oil, such as canola or safflower
1 small yellow onion, chopped
3 medium cloves garlic, minced
4 slices bacon, chopped
1 pound lean ground beef
2 tablespoons tomato paste
2 bay leaves
1 teaspoon smoked paprika

Kosher salt and freshly ground black pepper
1 cup dry white wine
1¾ cups chicken broth
¾ cup half-and-half or heavy cream
6 ounces (about 2 cups) elbow pasta
2 cups (about 8 ounces) shredded cheddar cheese
¼ cup chopped fresh parsley

1   Heat the oil in a 10-inch skillet over medium-low heat. Add the onions and cook until they turn a golden brown and begin to caramelize, stirring occasionally, about 15 minutes. Add the garlic and cook until fragrant, about 1 minute. Transfer the onion mixture to a bowl or plate and set aside.

2   Increase the heat to medium and add the bacon. Cook the bacon until the fat starts to render and the bacon begins to crisp, about 5 minutes. Add the beef, breaking it into small pieces with a large spoon, and cook until it browns, 5 to 7 minutes more. Remove from the heat and carefully drain off most of the fat from the skillet. Stir in the reserved onion mixture, tomato paste, bay leaves, paprika, and season to taste with salt and pepper.

3   Return your skillet to medium heat and add the wine. Reduce until almost dry, 3 to 5 minutes. Add the broth and half-and-half and bring to a boil. Add the pasta and return to a boil. Reduce the heat to a simmer and cook, covered, until the pasta is al dente, stirring frequently, about 10 minutes. Remove the bay leaves.

4   Reduce the heat to low and add the cheese, stirring until the cheese is completely melted and the sauce thickens. Fold in the parsley and serve.

REUBEN DUTCH BABY

This Dutch baby is no sweet sidekick; it is the real deal. With slices of savory pastrami layered over and under shredded Jarlsberg cheese, fresh herbs, and enough eggs to shake a carton at, it is equally at home as a full breakfast, lunch, or dinner. In fact, many of my friends have referred to this dish as a quiche because it is so hearty and egg-laden. The mustard and sauerkraut, with their acidic pop and bright flavors, really help to bring out the delicate flavors of the herbs, so don't forget to dollop them on the plate. Serve this Dutch baby with a side salad, slices of fresh fruit, or just on its own. Oh baby! Dutch baby.

MAKES 4 SERVINGS

1 cup plus 2 tablespoons all-purpose flour
½ teaspoon kosher salt
½ teaspoon freshly ground black pepper
8 large eggs
¾ cup whole milk
2 tablespoons minced fresh chives
1 teaspoon minced fresh thyme

1 teaspoon toasted caraway seeds
1 cup (about 4 ounces) shredded Jarlsberg cheese, divided
2 tablespoons unsalted butter
8 ounces thinly sliced pastrami, divided
Sauerkraut, for serving
Dijon or stone-ground mustard, for serving

1 Preheat the oven to 425 degrees F.
2 In a large bowl, whisk together the flour, salt, and pepper. In a separate bowl, whisk together the eggs and milk. Whisk the wet ingredients into the dry until just combined. Stir in the chives, thyme, caraway seeds, and half of the cheese.
3 Melt the butter in a 10-inch skillet over medium heat. Cook until it starts to brown and smells nutty, about 3 minutes. Swirl the skillet so the butter coats the bottom. Spread out half of the pastrami on the bottom of the skillet.
4 Pour the batter into your skillet on top of the pastrami. Transfer the skillet to the oven and bake until puffed and golden, about 25 minutes. Carefully remove the skillet from the oven and preheat the broiler.
5 Spread out the remaining pastrami over the Dutch baby and sprinkle with the remaining cheese. Broil until the cheese is melted, about 2 minutes. Serve immediately with the sauerkraut and mustard on the side.

TIP: If you have a hard time finding Jarlsberg cheese, Emmentaler, Swiss, or Gruyère are also pretty darn awesome in this dish.

HERB-CRUSTED FLANK STEAK

with Sauteed Grapes and Blue Cheese

This dish is as pretty to look at as it is to eat. And it's a real crowd-pleaser (but is easy enough for a weeknight dinner). Rich, flavorful, and quick-cooking flank steak is smothered in an herby-mustard sauce, then paired with sweet grapes and savory and salty blue cheese. (If you're not a fan of blue cheese, try a sprinkling of crumbled feta cheese instead.) For the biggest "wow factor," use a combination of different colored grapes, and snack on a few while cooking to keep hungry mouths at bay.

MAKES 4 SERVINGS

3 tablespoons high-heat oil, such as canola or safflower, divided
1 tablespoon chopped fresh rosemary
1 tablespoon Dijon mustard
1 (1½-pound) flank steak
Kosher salt and freshly ground black pepper

3 tablespoons dry white wine
5 medium shallots, thinly sliced
3 cups whole grapes, any color, halved
2 medium cloves garlic, minced
1 tablespoon balsamic vinegar
½ cup crumbled blue cheese
Crusty bread, for serving

1   In a small bowl, combine 1 tablespoon of the oil, the rosemary, and mustard. Set aside. Season both sides of the steak with salt and pepper.
2   Heat 1 tablespoon of the oil in a 10-inch skillet over medium heat. Cook the steak until it reaches an internal temperature of 135 degrees F (for medium-rare), 4 to 6 minutes per side, or to your desired degree of doneness. Spread half of the herb mixture on one side of the steak and cook for 1 additional minute. Flip the steak and spread the remaining herb mixture on the other side and cook for 1 minute. Transfer to a cutting board and tent loosely with aluminum foil.
3   Add the wine to the skillet and deglaze the pan, scraping up any browned bits with a wooden spoon. Add the remaining 1 tablespoon oil to the skillet. Cook the shallots until soft and golden, 7 to 9 minutes. Stir in the grapes and continue to cook until the grapes begin to soften, 5 to 6 minutes. Add the garlic and cook until fragrant, about 1 minute. Remove your skillet from the heat and stir in the vinegar. Season to taste with salt and pepper.
4   Thinly slice the steak against the grain. Arrange on a serving platter or individual plates and top with the grape mixture. Sprinkle the steak with the blue cheese and serve with slices of the crusty bread.

SKIRT STEAK STREET TACOS

with Corn and Black Bean Salad

This is the ultimate family meal because you can build your own tacos to suit your appetite. Choose how much spiced skirt steak, crisp and bright corn salad, and cream to add to your individual tacos. Some like even proportions, some prefer a higher meat-to-veggie ratio, and some prefer more veggies or even (gasp!) all veggies. I have given you a generous range of tortillas to purchase because it really depends on how you eat them. My kids will delicately nibble at two tacos with just a slice of steak (then proceed to eat a few more plain tortillas). My husband and I will wolf down four tacos stuffed to the gills before even thinking about it. Serrano peppers can have a bit of heat to them, so if you think your family or guests might shy away from spice, swap it out with another bell pepper.

MAKES 4 SERVINGS

1 tablespoon dark brown sugar
1½ teaspoons ground cumin
1½ teaspoons chili powder
1 teaspoon dried oregano
½ teaspoon ground coriander
¼ teaspoon ground cinnamon
1 (1½-pound) skirt steak, trimmed
Kosher salt and freshly ground
  black pepper
2 tablespoons high-heat oil, such as
  canola or safflower, divided
1 medium red bell pepper, diced
1 medium serrano pepper, seeded
  and diced

1 cup frozen corn, thawed
1 (15-ounce) can black beans, rinsed
  and drained
½ small red onion, diced
2 medium cloves garlic, minced
2 teaspoons fresh lime zest
2 tablespoons freshly squeezed
  lime juice
¼ cup chopped fresh cilantro
8 to 16 (4½-inch) "street taco" corn or
  flour tortillas, warmed
Mexican crema or sour cream,
  for serving
Lime wedges, for serving

1   In a small bowl, combine the brown sugar, cumin, chili powder, oregano, coriander, and cinnamon. Rub the steak with the spice mixture, cover, and refrigerate for at least 1 hour and up to 24 hours.

2   Remove the steak from the refrigerator and let it come to room temperature for 30 minutes. Season with salt and pepper.

3   Heat 1 tablespoon of the oil in a 10-inch skillet over medium heat. Add the steak and cook until well browned on the first side, 3 to 4 minutes. Flip the steak and continue to cook until well browned and it reaches an internal temperature of 135 degrees F (for medium-rare), 4 to 6 additional minutes. Transfer to a cutting board and tent loosely with aluminum foil.

4   Heat the remaining 1 tablespoon oil in your skillet over medium heat. Add the peppers, corn, black beans, and onions and cook until just softened, about 5 minutes. Add the garlic and cook for 1 minute. Stir in the lime zest, lime juice, and cilantro. Season to taste with salt and pepper.

5   Thinly slice the steak against the grain. Set out the taco components for guests to assemble, or serve the steak in the tortillas, topped with the corn salad and drizzled with the crema. Serve lime wedges alongside for squeezing.

SWAP IT OUT: Flank steak makes an excellent substitution for skirt steak in this recipe.

CLASSIC PATTY MELTS

with Caramelized Onions and Cheddar

What's the difference between a patty melt and a cheeseburger? The shape of your buns! Well, kind of. It's actually the shape of the patty (rectangular versus round) to fit on your buns (sliced bread versus a soft round bun). Both can be piled high with sweet, caramelized onions, plenty of cheese, and a smoky sauce. Traditionally, patty melts are served with Swiss cheese, but I just happen to prefer cheddar paired with the caramelized onions. It might sound weird to spread mayonnaise on the *outside* of your sandwich for cooking, but you've got to believe me . . . it results in the perfect golden crust, far superior to butter or oil. Give it a whirl, I think you will be pleasantly surprised.

MAKES 4 SERVINGS

3 tablespoons unsalted butter

2 medium sweet or yellow onions, thinly sliced

Kosher salt and freshly ground black pepper

1 pound lean ground beef

1 teaspoon Worcestershire sauce

1 teaspoon chopped fresh thyme, or ¼ teaspoon dried

3 tablespoons mayonnaise, plus more for cooking

2 tablespoons Dijon mustard

½ teaspoon smoked paprika

8 slices sourdough or pumpernickel bread

8 slices aged cheddar cheese

1 Melt the butter in a 10-inch skillet over medium-low heat. Add the onions and cook, stirring occasionally, until a deep golden brown, about 30 minutes. Season the onions to taste with salt and pepper, then remove them from the skillet. Wipe the skillet clean.

2 Meanwhile, in a large bowl, mix together the beef, Worcestershire, and thyme. Season to taste with salt and pepper. Divide the mixture into 4 portions and shape each into a ½-inch-thick square patty.

3 Cook the patties in your skillet over medium heat until browned and cooked through, about 3 minutes per side. Remove the patties from the skillet and wipe the skillet clean.

4 In a small bowl, mix together the mayonnaise, mustard, and paprika. Spread your desired amount of sauce on one side of each slice of bread. Top the bread slices with 1 slice of cheese, a hamburger patty, the onions, and a final slice of cheese. Top with the remaining bread, spread side down.

5 Spread a bit of mayonnaise on the outside of each slice of bread. Add two of the sandwiches to your skillet over low heat and cook until the bread is golden and the cheese is melted, 2 to 3 minutes per side. Repeat with the remaining sandwiches and serve immediately.

PAN-SEARED NEW YORK STEAK

with Tarragon Mustard and Spring Vegetables

The way to my husband's heart is steak and potatoes. I also make this dish when I want to impress the in-laws. The meal comes with an air of sophistication: crisp-tender fingerling potatoes, fresh asparagus, and peas, all drizzled with a tarragon-mustard sauce. The whole thing is topped with a killer steak. But in reality, it's a simple meal to make with basic ingredients. So I call it a win-win! Yes, this recipe calls for "spring" vegetables, but it can be made any time of the year. If you can't find fresh asparagus, which is rare no matter the season, swap it out with green beans. Fingerling potatoes are my personal favorite, but any kind of baby potatoes are absolutely delicious.

MAKES 4 SERVINGS

1½ to 2 pounds boneless New York steak
Kosher salt and freshly ground black
  pepper
¼ cup Dijon mustard
1 tablespoon sherry or red wine vinegar
1 tablespoon honey
¼ cup plus 3 tablespoons extra-virgin olive
  oil, divided

2 tablespoons chopped fresh tarragon
1 pound fingerling potatoes, sliced ¼ inch
  thick on the diagonal
1 small bunch thin asparagus spears (about
  1 pound), tough stems removed and
  stalks cut into 1-inch pieces
1 cup fresh or frozen and thawed peas
4 medium cloves garlic, minced

1   Season the steak with salt and pepper. Let it come to room temperature for
    30 minutes.
2   In a small bowl, whisk together the mustard, vinegar, and honey. Continue to whisk
    while slowly drizzing in ¼ cup of the oil to create an emulsified dressing. Fold in the
    tarragon and season to taste with salt and pepper. Set aside.
3   Heat 2 tablespoons of the oil in a 10-inch skillet over medium heat. Cook the steak
    until deep golden brown and it reaches an internal temperature of 135 degrees F (for
    medium-rare), flipping halfway through cooking, 10 to 12 minutes. Transfer to a cutting
    board and tent loosely with aluminum foil.
4   Heat the remaining 1 tablespoon oil in your skillet over medium heat. Add the potatoes
    and cook, stirring often, until golden and just tender, about 10 minutes. Add the
    asparagus and peas and cook until tender-crisp and warmed through, about 3 minutes.
    Stir in the garlic and cook until fragrant, 1 additional minute. Season to taste with salt
    and pepper. Remove from the heat and toss with half of the reserved mustard sauce.
5   Place the vegetables on a warmed serving platter. Slice the steak against the grain
    and shingle on top of the vegetables. Drizzle with the remaining mustard sauce and
    serve immediately.

SWAP IT OUT: Though nothing compares with New York steak, if you're budget-minded,
you can easily swap it out with tenderloin, skirt steak, or flank steak.

BEEF, GREEN BEAN, AND PINEAPPLE RED CURRY

Some folks like pineapple on their pizza, some like it in (or would that be *on*?) their upside-down cake, and I like it in my curry. I find it adds a touch of bright, acidic sweetness to this savory concoction with sirloin steak and green beans. If you prefer your curry mild, start with a tablespoon of paste. If you like it hot, double that up. If you can't find haricots verts (when not available fresh, sometimes they are in the freezer section), look for the thinnest green beans you can find. Thanks to the cultural traditions of my husband's family, we serve our curry with slices of fresh baguette instead of rice to soak up all of that amazing sauce. It may sound strange, but I encourage you to try it. You may never look back.

MAKES 4 SERVINGS

2 tablespoons cold water
2 teaspoons cornstarch
1 tablespoon sesame oil
1 pound sirloin or top round steak, trimmed and cut against the grain into ¼-inch-thick strips
1 to 2 tablespoons red curry paste
3 medium cloves garlic, minced
1 pound haricots verts (thin green beans), trimmed and cut in half

Kosher salt and freshly ground black pepper
1 (14-ounce) can unsweetened coconut milk
¾ cup chicken broth
1 (20-ounce) can pineapple chunks, drained
¼ cup fresh Thai basil leaves
Baguette, for serving

1   In a small bowl, mix together the water and cornstarch to make a slurry. Set aside.

2   Heat the oil in a 10-inch skillet over medium-high heat. Add the steak and cook, stirring, until browned, 2 to 4 minutes. Drain off any water or fat. Add the curry paste and garlic. Cook, stirring, until fragrant, about 1 minute. Stir in the haricots verts and season to taste with salt and pepper.

3   Pour in the coconut milk and broth; bring to a boil. Reduce to a simmer and cook, partially covered, until the green beans are just tender, about 8 minutes. Stir in the reserved cornstarch slurry and simmer, stirring gently, to thicken the sauce. Add the pineapple and season to taste with salt and pepper. Garnish with the basil and serve with the baguette for dipping.

SWAP IT OUT: If green beans aren't your thing, you can swap them out with an equal amount (in weight) of broccoli or fold in 5 ounces of baby spinach before adding the cornstarch slurry.

GOOD OL' BEEF POT PIE

My husband wouldn't let me write this book if I did not include this recipe. This is classic pot pie goodness: rich, hearty, and creamy. Beef and mushrooms, peas and carrots, gravy, and a sprinkling of cheese on top for good measure. And the best part is that most of the work is hands-off in your oven. I suggest that you use a good-quality red wine when preparing this dish so you have some for the pie and some for yourself, either while preparing the meal or to sip on while eating it. This is a pretty full skillet, so place it on a large rimmed baking sheet in the oven to avoid any spillover when stirring. As I've mentioned before, I'm not a pie-crust maker, so I always grab a frozen prepared crust from the store. But if you have the time and preference, feel free to make your own.

MAKES 6 SERVINGS

1 pound stew meat, trimmed and cut into ¾-inch cubes
Kosher salt and freshly ground black pepper
3 tablespoons high-heat oil, such as canola or safflower, divided
2 large carrots, chopped
8 ounces cremini mushrooms, stemmed and quartered
1 small yellow onion, chopped
2 tablespoons tomato paste
4 medium cloves garlic, minced

2 teaspoons chopped fresh thyme or oregano, or ½ teaspoon dried
½ cup dry red wine
2 tablespoons all-purpose flour
2 cups chicken broth
1 cup frozen and thawed peas
2 tablespoons chopped fresh parsley
1 egg
1 teaspoon water
1 prepared pie crust
¼ cup (about ¾ ounce) shredded Parmesan cheese

1   Preheat the oven to 400 degrees F with the rack positioned in the lower third of the oven.
2   Season the beef with salt and pepper. Heat 1 tablespoon of the oil in a 10-inch skillet over medium heat. Add the beef and cook until well browned on all sides, about 5 minutes. Transfer to a bowl and wipe the skillet clean.
3   Add the remaining 2 tablespoons oil to your skillet over medium heat. Add the carrots, mushrooms, and onions. Cook until softened and lightly browned, 5 to 7 minutes. Stir in the tomato paste, garlic, and thyme, and cook until fragrant, about 1 minute. Season to taste with salt and pepper. Add the wine to the skillet and cook until almost completely evaporated, 1 to 2 minutes. Stir in the flour and cook for 1 additional minute.

4   Slowly stir in the broth, scraping up any browned bits from your skillet and smoothing out any lumps. Return the beef and any accumulated juices to your skillet and bring to a simmer. Cover with an ovenproof lid or piece of aluminum foil and transfer the skillet to the oven. Cook until the beef is almost tender, about 30 minutes, stirring halfway through. Carefully remove your skillet from the oven and stir in the peas and parsley.

5   In a small bowl, whisk together the egg and water. Unroll the pie crust and place it on top of the hot filling, crimping the edges if necessary. Cut four small vents in the top to release steam. Lightly brush the egg wash over the crust and sprinkle with the Parmesan.

6   Return your skillet to the oven and continue to bake until the filling is bubbly and the crust is golden brown, 20 to 25 minutes. Let stand for 20 minutes before serving.

SWAP IT OUT: Cremini mushrooms are just baby portobellos. You can also use plain old white button mushrooms, which are widely available and will taste equally delicious.

ROOT VEGETABLE AND BEEF SKILLET GRATIN

Don't get me wrong: I love shepherd's pie, but I despise making mashed potatoes. It's so much work to boil the potatoes, mash them, then clean everything up afterward. My version of shepherd's pie goes with slices instead of mash, and decidedly more cheese. And those slices aren't just potatoes—they're a root vegetable gratin (another of my favorite dishes). So here we are: savory beef layered with, well . . . layers of rutabagas and potatoes. The whole thing is smothered in cheese and cream, then baked until tender perfection. Make sure you place your skillet on a sheet pan to catch any cheese and cream bubble-ups-and-overs while baking.

MAKES 4 TO 6 SERVINGS

2 tablespoons extra-virgin olive oil, divided
1 pound lean ground beef
Kosher salt and freshly ground black pepper
1 small yellow onion, thinly sliced
4 medium cloves garlic, minced
1½ teaspoons dried oregano
5 ounces baby spinach

2 small Yukon gold potatoes (about 1 pound), sliced ⅛ inch thick
1 medium rutabaga (about 1 pound), peeled and sliced ⅛ inch thick
2 cups (about 4 ounces) shredded Gruyère cheese, divided
½ cup heavy cream
½ cup (about 1½ ounces) shredded Parmesan cheese

1   Preheat the oven to 350 degrees F with the rack positioned in the lower third of the oven.

2   Heat 1 tablespoon of the oil in a 10-inch skillet over medium heat. Add the beef, breaking it into small pieces with a large spoon, and brown well, 7 to 9 minutes. Season to taste with salt and pepper. Drain the beef and transfer it to a plate. Drain any fat from the skillet and wipe it clean with a paper towel.

3   Heat the remaining 1 tablespoon oil in your skillet over medium heat. Add the onions and cook until softened, stirring occasionally, about 5 minutes. Stir in the garlic and oregano and cook until fragrant, about 1 minute. Add the spinach, a handful at a time, stirring until wilted, about 3 minutes. Season to taste with salt and pepper. Remove your skillet from the heat and fold in the reserved beef.

4   Layer half the potato and rutabaga slices over the meat mixture, alternating rutabaga and potato slices, with each slice slightly overlapping another. Season lightly with salt and pepper and sprinkle with half the Gruyère cheese.

Repeat with the remaining vegetables and Gruyère cheese. Pour the cream over the top.

5   Place the skillet on a baking sheet and cover it tightly with aluminum foil or an ovenproof lid. Bake until the vegetables are very tender, 50 to 60 minutes. Carefully remove the skillet from the oven and sprinkle the top with the Parmesan cheese.

6   Preheat the broiler with the rack 6 inches from the element. Return the skillet to the oven and broil until the cheese is melted and the top is golden brown, 2 to 4 minutes. Let cool for 10 minutes before serving.

SWAP IT OUT: If you're not a fan of rutabaga, swap it with an equal weight of parsnips, turnips, kohlrabi, or more potatoes.

SPICED BEEF AND CHICKPEA-STUFFED PITAS "KAWARMA"

The dinner where sloppy Joes meets falafel sandwich meets kawarma. A Lebanese dish, kawarma is usually a side dish of hummus topped with fried ground lamb. In this version, I left the hummus unsmooshed (whole chickpeas) and swapped out the lamb with beef (although lamb would make an excellent substitution). It's a bit spiced (in the flavorful, not hot, way), a bit sweet (thanks to currants and cinnamon), and a bit fresh (thanks to herbs). And the whole thing fits in a nice little pocket (of pita bread). For a bit of added crunch, throw some sliced cucumbers or thinly sliced red onions into the pita if you happen to have any in the fridge.

MAKES 4 SERVINGS

1 tablespoon extra-virgin olive oil
1 pound lean ground beef
1 (15-ounce) can chickpeas, rinsed and drained
1 tablespoon tomato paste
3 medium cloves garlic, minced
1 teaspoon ground cumin
1 teaspoon ground coriander
½ teaspoon ground cinnamon
½ teaspoon smoked paprika
Kosher salt and freshly ground black pepper
1 cup chicken broth or water
¼ cup currants
2 tablespoons chopped fresh mint
2 tablespoons chopped fresh cilantro
4 to 8 pita breads, sliced in half
4 large lettuce leaves
1 large tomato, sliced
Plain Greek yogurt, for serving

1   Heat the oil in a 10-inch skillet over medium heat. Add the beef, breaking it into small pieces with a large spoon, and cook until just browned, about 8 minutes. Drain off any extra fat or liquid. Stir in the chickpeas and continue to cook, stirring occasionally, until the chickpeas start to brown slightly, about 8 minutes more. If the mixture begins to scorch the bottom of the skillet, reduce the heat a little and add a splash of water.

2   Add the tomato paste, garlic, cumin, coriander, cinnamon, and paprika and cook until fragrant, about 1 minute. Season to taste with salt and pepper. Stir in the broth and currants, scraping the bottom of the skillet to loosen any browned bits. Reduce the heat to medium-low and cook until the mixture is almost dry, about 5 minutes. Fold in the mint and cilantro.

3   Spoon the mixture into the pita bread and add the lettuce leaves and sliced tomatoes. Dollop with the yogurt and serve immediately.

SWAP IT OUT: If you don't have currants on hand, golden or regular raisins make an excellent substitution.

SEARED RIB-EYE STEAK

with Wilted Napa Cabbage

Sometimes simple is better. Juicy and tender rib-eye steak is cooked in a hot skillet until perfectly medium-rare (this is what skillets are made for, after all), then smothered in a buttery garlic-ginger sauce that has a hint of sweetness from hoisin. Yes, you can cook the steak to a different doneness, but just don't tell me about it. A bright and crunchy mixture of shredded cabbage and carrots is then cooked in the same skillet until warm and wilted in that same amazing sauce and served alongside that amazing steak. It's somewhat fancy, super delicious, and ridiculously easy to prepare. This is the type of dish where you do want to splurge on a nice cut of beef, because it cooks quickly. If rib-eye is not your thing, look for T-bone, filet mignon, or porterhouse. If you do want to save a few dollars, flat iron and tri-tip sirloin steaks are a safe (and delicious) bet.

MAKES 4 SERVINGS

1½ pounds rib-eye steak, about 1¼ inch thick
Kosher salt and freshly ground black pepper
1 tablespoon sesame oil
2 tablespoons unsalted butter
1 tablespoon minced peeled fresh ginger
2 medium cloves garlic, minced

2 tablespoons hoisin sauce
1 small head Napa cabbage (about 1 pound), thinly shredded
2 large carrots, peeled and shredded
¼ cup dry white wine
1 tablespoon soy sauce
2 teaspoons toasted sesame seeds
Dash of chili oil (optional)

1   Season the steak with salt and pepper and let it come to room temperature for 30 minutes.

2   Heat the oil in a 10-inch skillet over medium heat. Add the steak and cook until it reaches an internal temperature of 135 degrees F (for medium-rare), 5 to 7 minutes per side. Transfer to a cutting board and tent loosely with aluminum foil.

3   Add the butter, ginger, and garlic to the pan and cook for 30 seconds. Stir in the hoisin sauce. Return the steaks to the skillet and cook on each side for an additional 30 seconds to coat with the sauce. Return the steaks to the cutting board, cover with aluminum foil, and let rest while cooking the cabbage.

4   Add the cabbage, carrots, and wine to the pan and cook, stirring, until the cabbage is wilted, about 3 to 5 minutes. Sprinkle it with the soy sauce, sesame seeds, and chili oil.

5   Place the cabbage mixture on a warmed serving platter. Thinly slice the steak against the grain and place it on top of the cabbage; serve immediately.

NOT QUITE KOSHER:
Pork Recipes

I'll be honest, I didn't grow up eating a lot of pork in my family. Not just because we were of a certain religious persuasion (we did regularly go out for dim sum with my parents and Bubbe, and y'all know that everything stuffed into those amazing rolling carts does not fall in the kosher category). But because, for whatever reason, my mom was "afraid" (her word, not mine) to cook pork. Maybe it was the lack of exposure to pork herself growing up? Maybe it was an overwhelming feeling of Jewish guilt that prevented her from cooking *treif* food in our home, thinking God might smite her (but it was somehow totally OK to eat pig and shellfish outside the home, and with gusto)? Maybe it was just one less thing she wanted to add to the weekly grocery shopping list with three kids in tow? We may never know (well, she just may never tell us).

Suffice it to say, the lack of piggie in my childhood did not affect my love for bacon (and all other things pork related) as an adult. You'll find a half hog in my chest freezer out in the garage, and my folks come over often for breakfast, lunch, and dinner asking for an extra slice of bacon, a double serving of pork chops, or to please pass another hum bao. Whether you're cooking up these recipes yourself or encouraging your family members to cook them up for you, I think you'll be delighted to discover that cooking pork is no big deal. Plus, with just one skillet, it's also pretty darn easy to clean up afterward. From bacon to sausage to chops to grind, you'll find all things swine perfectly fine.

PORK CHOPS

with Cashew-Lime Rice

Both the hubby and the tween consider this dish to be a "winner." Which on one hand is super sweet and makes me thrilled that a majority of the household is happy to eat the same dish at the same time. On the other hand, it makes me question . . . Wait. Are not all of my dishes winners? What gives?

This dish is fusion food at its best. With oregano and tomato stirred into the rice, it reminds me of traveling in Mexico. However, it's also reminiscent of our time in Thailand, with bright lime flavors, salty and crunchy cashews, and a ton of fresh herbs. I guess it's the dish I make when I'm wanting to travel or fondly daydreaming of times when we're able to escape responsibilities. Which is funny, since it's a quick and easy dinner to whip together to feed all of those responsibilities.

MAKES 4 SERVINGS

4 (¾- to 1-inch-thick) boneless pork chops, trimmed

Kosher salt and freshly ground black pepper

3 tablespoons high-heat oil, such as canola or safflower, divided

½ medium yellow onion, finely chopped

1 medium jalapeño pepper, seeded and finely chopped (optional)

3 medium cloves garlic, minced

1 tablespoon tomato paste

1 teaspoon dried oregano

¼ teaspoon ground coriander

1 cup long-grain white rice, such as jasmine or basmati

2 cups chicken broth

¼ cup roughly chopped fresh cilantro, divided

1 tablespoon honey

3 tablespoons freshly squeezed lime juice

2 teaspoons fresh lime zest

4 green onions, white and green parts chopped

½ cup roughly chopped salted roasted cashews

1 Season each pork chop with salt and pepper.

2 Heat 1 tablespoon of the oil in a 10-inch skillet over medium heat. Add the chops and brown well on one side only, for about 5 minutes. Transfer the chops to a plate.

3 Pour off all but 1 tablespoon fat from the skillet. Add the onions and jalapeño pepper and cook until soft and translucent, about 5 minutes. Stir in the garlic, tomato paste, oregano, and coriander. Cook until aromatic, about 30 seconds. Add the rice and stir to coat. Season lightly with salt and pepper.

4 Pour the broth into the pan and stir to evenly distribute the rice. Bring to a simmer. Nestle the chops, brown side up, in the rice. Reduce the heat to low and cover. Gently simmer until the chops reach an internal temperature of 145 degrees F and the flesh is firm when prodded with a finger, 6 to 8 minutes.

→

5   Remove the chops from the skillet and transfer to a cutting board. Loosely tent with aluminum foil and let rest while the rice continues to cook.

6   Stir the rice and continue to cook, covered, on low heat until the rice is tender and the liquid is absorbed, 10 to 12 minutes more.

7   In a small bowl, whisk the remaining 2 tablespoons oil, half the cilantro, the honey, lime juice, and lime zest. Season to taste with salt and pepper.

8   When the rice is cooked, remove the skillet from the heat and fold in the remaining cilantro, the green onions, and cashews. Divide the rice among four bowls. Slice the pork into strips and arrange on top of the rice. Drizzle with the vinaigrette and serve.

TIP: Does your pork curl while cooking? Before searing it in your skillet, cut two slits, about 2 inches apart, on the fat of each chop. This gives the fat a little wiggle room to keep them flat once they hit the heat.

"THE KIDS' FAVORITE" SKILLET LASAGNA

We are big fans of lasagna in my family. Noodles, sauce, a bit of meat, and all of that creamy, cheesy goodness. However, as much as I'm a fan of eating the stuff, I'm not really a fan of cooking it. There's just too much time involved making sauce, parboiling noodles, creating beautiful but repetitive layers, and then you still have to bake the darn thing for an hour. I want to cook dinner and be done with it. Enter stage left: skillet lasagna. All of the same great flavors and textures, but like fifteen minutes of actual work. The aromatics and pork are cooked together, sprinkled with pasta, and covered with a quick and easy sauce (pop a can or open a jar . . . dealer's choice). The pasta absorbs a ton of flavor as it simmers in the ad hoc sauce, then finally the whole thing is smothered in cheese. The best part is that it's ready to eat in just thirty minutes.

MAKES 6 SERVINGS

1 tablespoon extra-virgin olive oil
1 large carrot, diced
½ medium yellow onion, diced
3 medium cloves garlic, minced
1 tablespoon Italian herb seasoning
Pinch of red pepper flakes (optional)
½ pound ground pork
¼ cup roughly chopped fresh basil
Kosher salt and freshly ground black
  pepper

6 ounces (1½ to 2 cups) conchiglie shells
  or farfalle pasta
1½ cups chicken broth or water
1 (15-ounce) can crushed tomatoes
1 cup marinara sauce
1½ cups (about 6 ounces) shredded
  mozzarella cheese
½ cup (about 1½ ounces) shredded
  Parmesan cheese

1   Heat the oil in a 10-inch skillet over medium heat. Add the carrots and onions and cook until tender, 5 to 7 minutes. Stir in the garlic, Italian herbs, and red pepper flakes and cook for 1 minute. Add the ground pork, breaking it into small pieces with a wooden spoon, and cook until browned, about 5 minutes. Fold in the basil and season to taste with salt and pepper.

2   Scatter the pasta over the pork. Pour the broth, tomatoes, and marinara sauce over the top; stir well to combine. Bring to a boil, cover, and reduce to a simmer. Cook, stirring occasionally, until the pasta is tender, about 20 minutes. Remove from the heat.

3   Sprinkle the cheeses on top of the pasta and cover the pan. Let rest for 5 minutes to allow the cheese to melt. Or place the skillet under the broiler for 2 to 3 minutes to melt and brown the cheese.

SWAP IT OUT: Bulk turkey sausage or ground beef make excellent substitutes for the pork.

GRITS-CRUSTED HAM AND CHEESE QUICHE

This dish is comfort food at its finest. Creamy and cheesy grits baked into a "crust," then topped with crisp ham, more cheese, and finally a rich egg custard. It takes a little elbow grease to prepare, but it is well worth the effort. One might consider it more of a breakfast dish, but we eat it for dinner on a regular basis. We've also been known to actually eat it for breakfast, when there happens to be a slice left over. But let's just say that's a rare occurrence.

   This recipe is best made in a well-seasoned skillet. The grits crust can leave a bit of mess behind in your pan, once the meal has been eaten. But if you've taken care of your skillet, any remnants should easily wipe out with a plastic scrubber or brush and a bit of warm water. Though most of us are used to whisking grits, I recommend stirring with a wooden spoon. We wouldn't want a metal whisk to undo all of our hard seasoning work now, would we?

MAKES 6 SERVINGS

6 ounces ham steak, chopped (see tip)
2 medium cloves garlic, minced
3 cups low-fat milk
2 tablespoons unsalted butter
¾ cup old-fashioned grits
1½ cups (about 6 ounces) shredded cheddar cheese, divided

Kosher salt and freshly ground black pepper
Pinch of cayenne pepper
6 large eggs, divided
⅔ cup half-and-half or heavy cream
4 green onions, white and green parts sliced

1   Preheat the oven to 350 degrees F.
2   Heat a 10-inch skillet over medium heat. Add the ham and cook until just crisp, about 4 minutes. Stir in the garlic and cook for 1 additional minute. Remove the ham using a slotted spoon and drain on paper towels. Reserve any drippings in the skillet.
3   Add the milk and butter to the skillet; bring to a boil over high heat. Slowly stir in the grits with a wooden spoon. Reduce the heat to medium-low and cook at a simmer, stirring constantly, until the grits are very thick, about 7 minutes. Remove from the heat and stir in 1 cup of the cheese until smooth. Season to taste with salt, black pepper, and cayenne pepper. Let cool for 5 minutes, then stir in 2 beaten eggs until well blended.
4   Bake the grits in the oven until set, about 20 minutes. Carefully remove the skillet from the oven and reduce the oven temperature to 325 degrees F.

5 Whisk together the remaining 4 eggs and the half-and-half in a bowl. Season to taste with salt and pepper.

6 Sprinkle the grits crust with the reserved ham, remaining ½ cup cheese, and the green onions (I like to smoosh it all down a bit into the grits). Slowly pour the egg mixture over the top.

7 Return your skillet to the oven and bake until the center is set and the top is lightly browned, 35 to 45 minutes. Let stand for 20 minutes before serving.

TIP: Ham steak is also sometimes referred to as "country ham." Basically, any nice thick slab of ham will do. And if no ham is to be found, swap it out with bacon or leftover pork chops.

MUSTARD-COATED PORK TENDERLOIN

with Green Beans and Potatoes

A mostly hands-off recipe, featuring mostly common ingredients found in your pantry or fridge, for a mostly easy weeknight dinner. That's a winner in my book (and . . . this *is* my book!). A majority of the work for this comforting dinner happens in the oven, with just a little bit of effort needed from the chef in the beginning. And the final results are a savory and tender pork loin, with all the fixings. Depending on how your tenderloin arrives from the store, market, or farm, you may need to cut it in half or thirds (crosswise, or "hamburger" style, not "hot dog" style, as I remember it from kindergarten) to fit in your skillet.

MAKES 4 SERVINGS

¼ cup stone-ground mustard
2 tablespoons chopped fresh parsley
2 medium cloves garlic, minced
1 tablespoon freshly squeezed lemon juice, plus more as needed
1 tablespoon honey
1 pound fingerling potatoes, halved lengthwise if small or quartered if large

1 tablespoon high-heat oil, such as canola or safflower
Kosher salt and freshly ground black pepper
1½ pounds pork tenderloin, trimmed and halved
½ pound green beans, trimmed and cut into 2-inch lengths

1 Preheat the oven to 450 degrees F with the rack in the lower-middle position.
2 In a small bowl, combine the mustard, parsley, garlic, lemon juice, and honey. Reserve 3 tablespoons of the mustard mixture in a separate small bowl. Set both bowls aside.
3 In a 10-inch skillet, toss together the potatoes and oil. Season to taste with salt and pepper. Place the skillet in your oven and roast the potatoes for 10 minutes.
4 Meanwhile, pat the tenderloins dry with paper towels and season with salt and pepper. Brush the top with the larger portion of the mustard mixture. Carefully remove the skillet from the oven and toss the potatoes. Lay the tenderloins on top of the potatoes. Roast until the tenderloins reach an internal temperature of 145 degrees F or the juices run clear when the tenderloin is poked with a knife, 30 to 40 minutes.
5 Carefully remove the skillet from the oven and transfer the tenderloins to a cutting board. Tent loosely with aluminum foil.
6 Add the green beans to the skillet and gently toss with the potatoes and the remaining 3 tablespoons of the mustard mixture. Return your skillet to the oven and continue to roast until the vegetables are tender and golden, 10 to 15 additional minutes. Carefully remove the skillet from the oven and squeeze with additional lemon juice and salt and pepper to taste.
7 Slice the pork into ½-inch-thick slices on the diagonal and serve on top of the vegetables.

BACON AND POBLANO GRILLED CHEESE

Well, this may not be one of the healthiest recipes in this book, I will admit, but it is hella tasty. Smoky bacon is layered with provolone cheese and roasted poblano peppers. Of course, all of the steps are easily completed in your cast iron skillet, from roasting to frying to grilling. Roasting the peppers in your skillet gives them a great char and a hint of smoke, without leaving your stove top a complete mess (or having to fire up the grill). If you're feeling super decadent, swap out the provolone with Brie cheese. And don't scoff at the mayo on the *outside* of the sandwich—it helps get that absolutely perfect golden crust. Though this sandwich is fantastic on its own, it wouldn't really be a complete meal without a bowl of steaming hot tomato soup served alongside.

MAKES 4 SERVINGS

4 medium poblano peppers
8 to 12 slices bacon (see tip)
8 slices sourdough sandwich bread

16 slices provolone cheese
Mayonnaise, for spreading

1   Heat a 10-inch skillet over medium heat and add the poblano peppers. Cook, turning occasionally, until charred on all sides, 15 to 20 minutes. Place the peppers in a small bowl and cover with plastic wrap. Let cool for 5 minutes. Using your hands, peel the skin from the peppers. Split the peppers lengthwise and discard the stem and seeds. (Do not rinse the peppers under water, simply rub all of the seeds off with your hands.)

2   Heat your skillet over medium heat and add the bacon, working in batches if needed. Cook until crisp, flipping occasionally, 7 to 10 minutes. Remove the bacon from the skillet and drain on paper towels. Drain the fat from the skillet and wipe it clean with a paper towel.

3   Layer 4 slices of bread with 2 slices of cheese, 2 to 3 slices bacon, 1 roasted pepper, then top with 2 more slices of cheese. Top with the remaining bread. Brush the outside of each piece of bread with mayonnaise.

4   Heat your skillet over low heat. Add 2 sandwiches and cook until the cheese is melted and the bread is toasted, 3 to 4 minutes per side. Repeat with the remaining sandwiches. Serve immediately.

TIP: Why the range in bacon? Some bacon is thin, some is chunky. Some like a lot (yes, please!), some like a little (I'll eat yours). So add as much or as little bacon as you and your sandwich desire.

PORK RAMEN

with Bamboo and Mushrooms

This is the case of the magical disappearing broth. An aromatic soup base is made of pork drippings, shiitake mushrooms, garlic, and ginger, then topped off with chicken broth and oyster sauce. Plain old ramen noodles (yep, the kind you buy ten for a dollar at the supermarket) are placed in this magical elixir, then voilà! Six minutes later there's no broth, and those cheap-ass noodles have been transformed into something beyond imagination, but definitely not beyond scarfing down, as they absorb all those amazing flavors while cooking. This ramen bowl is easily customizable. Throw in corn, edamame, or any other fresh, frozen, or leftover veggies you like. Or top it with kombu flakes or strips of nori seaweed.

MAKES 4 SERVINGS

3 teaspoons water

¼ teaspoon baking soda

1 pound boneless country-style pork ribs, trimmed and sliced thin

3 tablespoons soy sauce, divided

1 teaspoon cornstarch

3 tablespoons sesame oil, divided

8 ounces shiitake mushrooms, stemmed and thinly sliced

6 green onions, white and green parts separated and thinly sliced

1 (8-ounce) can sliced bamboo shoots, drained

4 medium cloves garlic, minced

1 teaspoon minced peeled fresh ginger

Pinch of red pepper flakes (optional)

3 cups chicken broth

2 tablespoons oyster or hoisin sauce

3 (3-ounce) packages ramen noodles, seasoning packets discarded

Sambal oelek or chili paste, for serving (optional)

1   In a medium bowl, combine the water and baking soda. Add the pork and toss to coat; let sit for 5 minutes. Add 1 tablespoon of the soy sauce and the cornstarch and toss to combine.

2   Heat 1 tablespoon of the oil in a 10-inch skillet over medium-high heat. Drain any excess liquid from the pork. Add the pork in a single layer and cook, without stirring, until browned on the bottom, about 2 minutes. Stir and continue to cook until the pork is cooked through, 2 to 3 additional minutes. Transfer to a clean bowl and drain any fat or liquid from the skillet.

3   Heat the remaining 2 tablespoons oil in the skillet over medium heat. Add the mushrooms and a splash of water and cook until they start to release their juices, 3 to 5 minutes. Stir in the green onion whites, bamboo shoots, garlic, ginger, and red pepper flakes. Cook until fragrant, about 1 minute.

→

4   Stir in the broth, oyster sauce, and remaining 2 tablespoons soy sauce. Bring to a boil. Place the noodles in an even layer in your skillet, breaking them into smaller pieces if necessary. Cover the skillet, reduce the heat to medium-low, and simmer until the noodle bottoms have softened, about 3 minutes.

5   Using tongs, carefully flip the noodles over and gently stir to separate. Stir in the green onions greens and continue to cook until the noodles are tender, about 2 minutes more. Stir the pork and any accumulated juices into the skillet and cook until heated through, about 30 seconds. Serve with the sambal oelek.

TIP: If you can't find boneless country-style pork ribs, pork tenderloin or boneless pork chops will do in a pinch.

CHORIZO AND SWEET POTATO QUESADILLAS

I could eat quesadillas every single day and be perfectly happy. They are easy to make, endlessly versatile, and oddly comforting. They are my "ride or die" meal. This particular quesadilla, stuffed with chorizo, mashed sweet potatoes, and more cheese than you can shake a stick at, is a full meal smooshed between two tortillas. And yes, it's perfectly suitable for breakfast, lunch, or dinner. Or all three, if you're anything like me. Speaking of chorizo . . . this recipe calls for the Spanish dry-cured variety, not the fresh Mexican style. Technically, it's ready to snack on without cooking, but I just like how it releases some yummy oils into the pan to cook the potatoes in. Look for the cured chorizo alongside other dried and cured sausage, like cured salami or coppa, not the fresh stuff kept in the refrigerated section. And if you can't find Spanish chorizo, go ahead and use some salami or coppa!

MAKES 4 SERVINGS

8 ounces Spanish-style dry-cured chorizo, cut into ¼-inch cubes

½ to 1 tablespoon high-heat oil, such as canola or safflower

1 medium sweet potato (about 4 ounces), cut into ¼-inch cubes

Kosher salt and freshly ground black pepper

8 (8-inch) flour tortillas

4 green onions, white and green parts thinly sliced

2 cups (about 8 ounces) mozzarella cheese

1 cup (about 5 ounces) crumbled queso fresco

Sour cream, for serving

1   Preheat the oven to 200 degrees F. Place a wire rack on a baking sheet.

2   Heat a 10-inch skillet over medium heat. Add the chorizo and cook until browned and the fat begins to render, stirring often, about 8 minutes. Remove the chorizo using a slotted spoon and drain on paper towels.

3   If there is not a lot of rendered fat in the pan, add enough oil to the skillet to equal about 1 tablespoon of combined oil/fat. Add the sweet potatoes. Cook, stirring often, until the potatoes are charred and tender, about 10 minutes. Season to taste with salt and pepper. Remove from the skillet and mash.

4   Set out 4 tortillas on a work surface. Spread evenly with the sweet potato mash, then scatter the chorizo and green onions over the top of each. Sprinkle with the cheeses and top with the remaining tortillas.

5   Heat your skillet over low heat. Carefully place one quesadilla in the skillet and cook until lightly browned, about 4 minutes. Flip and cook until the second side is browned and the cheese is melted, about 3 minutes. Keep your quesadillas warm while you make the next round by placing the cooked quesadillas in a single layer on the wire rack on the baking sheet in the oven.

6   Cut the quesadillas into wedges and serve with the sour cream.

TIP: Some like to make their quesadillas "dry" (author raises her hand) and some "wet" for a bit of sheen (author's husband raises his hand). If you like a dry quesadilla, simply place it in your skillet and melt away. If you like it with a little sheen, add a touch more oil or a bit of butter to the skillet before cooking. Which should you choose? That's up to you. But if you live in a divided household and are making multiple quesadillas, start with the dry version, then cook the wet.

CARAWAY-CRUSTED PORK TENDERLOIN

with Sauerkraut and Apples

Whenever I can come up with an excuse to eat sauerkraut, I do it. I'm not sure what it is about the stuff . . . the crunchy cabbage, the funky fermentation, a deep ancestral calling to my roots. I can't get enough of it. Combine that with caramelized onions, sweet-tart apples, a perfectly roasted pork tenderloin, and then top the whole thing off with a proverbial (savory and spicy) icing on the cake (mustard—my condiment of choice) . . . Basically, this is perfection served in a skillet.

MAKES 4 SERVINGS

1 pound pork tenderloin, trimmed and halved
2 tablespoons caraway seeds
Kosher salt and freshly ground black pepper
2 tablespoons high-heat oil, such as canola or safflower, divided
1 small yellow onion, thinly sliced

2 sweet-tart apples, such as Honeycrisp or Gala, cored, halved, and sliced ¼ inch thick
3 medium cloves garlic, minced
2 tablespoons dark brown sugar
1 tablespoon champagne or white wine vinegar
1 (16-ounce) jar sauerkraut, drained
2 tablespoons chopped fresh parsley
Dijon or stone-ground mustard, for serving

1 Preheat the oven to 450 degrees F.
2 Pat the tenderloins dry with paper towels. Coat the surface with the caraway seeds and season with salt and pepper.
3 Heat 1 tablespoon of the oil in a 10-inch skillet over medium heat. Brown the tenderloins on all sides, 5 to 7 minutes. Transfer to a plate.
4 Add the remaining 1 tablespoon oil to your skillet over medium heat. Add the onions and cook until soft, about 5 minutes. Add the apples and continue to cook until soft and golden, another 5 minutes. Stir in the garlic, sugar, and vinegar and cook for 30 seconds. Fold in the sauerkraut. Season to taste with salt and pepper.
5 Place the tenderloins on the sauerkraut mixture and transfer your skillet to the oven. Roast until the pork reaches an internal temperature of 145 degrees F or the juices run clear when the tenderloins are poked with a knife, 15 to 20 minutes. Carefully remove the skillet from the oven and let the pork rest for 5 minutes before slicing ½ inch thick. Stir the parsley into the sauerkraut mixture and serve with the sliced pork with the mustard on the side.

TIP: Sauerkraut comes in all kinds of amazing flavors nowadays: spicy, sweet; heck, some of them aren't even made with cabbage. For this dish, keep it simple and stick with classic kraut for the best flavor.

YAM AND BEET HASH

with Italian Sausage

Is it breakfast? Is it dinner? It's all the things you need in a delicious anytime meal. Yams and beets are pan-roasted until caramelized and tender, then tossed with a bit of fresh kale, wine, and mildly sweet-savory sausage. Top the whole thing off with a few eggs, and this becomes the breakfast-dinner of champions. It's also not too shabby to look at, with its striking orange, red, green, and white colors. I like a dash or two of hot sauce (because whenever I have eggs, I *must* have hot sauce) on top, but to each their own.

MAKES 4 SERVINGS

3 tablespoons high-heat oil, such as canola or safflower, divided
½ medium yellow onion, thinly sliced
½ pound mild or hot bulk Italian sausage
2 medium garnet or jewel yams (about 1 pound), scrubbed and cut into ½-inch cubes
2 medium red or golden beets (about 1 pound), peeled and cut into ½-inch cubes
4 medium cloves garlic, minced

1 teaspoon chopped fresh thyme
1 teaspoon fennel seeds
Kosher salt and freshly ground black pepper
1 large bunch lacinato kale (about 8 ounces), tough stems removed and leaves chopped
¾ cup dry white wine, chicken broth, or water
4 large eggs

1   Heat 1 tablespoon of the oil in a 10-inch skillet over medium heat. Cook the onions until soft, about 5 minutes. Add the sausage; cook and crumble until browned, 7 to 9 minutes. Remove the sausage and onions from the pan and set aside.

2   Heat the remaining 2 tablespoons oil in your skillet over medium heat. Add the yams and beets and cook, stirring occasionally, until golden and just tender, about 15 minutes. Stir in the garlic, thyme, and fennel seeds, and cook for 1 additional minute. Season to taste with salt and pepper.

3   Reduce the heat to low. Stir in the kale and wine and cook, covered, stirring occasionally, until the kale is wilted and the yams and beets are tender, 5 to 7 minutes.

4   Return the sausage mixture to the skillet and stir to incorporate. Use a large spoon to create four small wells in the hash. Crack 1 egg into each well. Cover and cook until the whites are set, about 8 minutes. Serve immediately.

TIP: No need to peel the yams, the skin will cook up perfectly fine (but do make sure to give them a good scrub first). Definitely peel the beets—either with a peeler or using a knife—since their skin is not as appetizing.

SUPER-FANCY BACON AND PORCINI SKILLET NACHOS

Just like preparing for a hike during the springtime, you need to approach this dish with layers in mind. It might seem like a bit of work, but be sure to make four layers of chips-mushrooms-cheese so every piece of tortilla chip gets an equal slathering of toppings (not a dry chip in the house, y'all).

MAKES 6 SERVINGS

6 slices bacon, chopped
½ small red onion, sliced
8 ounces porcini mushrooms, stemmed and thinly sliced
High-heat oil, such as canola or safflower, as needed for sautéing
3 medium cloves garlic, minced
Pinch of red pepper flakes

5 ounces baby spinach
Truffle or kosher salt and freshly ground black pepper
1 (9-ounce) bag corn tortilla chips, divided
4 ounces (2 to 3 cups) shredded Fontina or Gouda cheese, divided
Crème fraîche, for serving

1   Preheat the oven to 400 degrees F.
2   Heat a 10-inch skillet over medium heat. Add the bacon and cook until it starts to crisp and the fat renders a bit, about 5 minutes. Add the onions and mushrooms and cook until the onions are soft and the mushrooms have released their juices, 5 to 7 minutes, adding a touch of oil if needed. Stir in the garlic and red pepper flakes and cook until fragrant, about 1 minute.
3   Add the spinach, a large handful at a time, and cook until wilted, about 4 minutes. Season to taste with salt and pepper. Transfer the mixture to a plate.
4   Spread one-quarter of the tortilla chips in the skillet. Sprinkle with one-quarter of the cheese and one-quarter of the mushroom mixture. Repeat the layers three more times with the remaining ingredients.
5   Bake in the oven until the cheese is melted, about 10 minutes. Serve with the crème fraîche for dipping.

SWAP IT OUT: No porcinis? No problem. Simply swap them out with shiitake or even cremini mushrooms.

SESAME PORK CUTLETS
with Warm Mustard Greens

You're never supposed to pick a favorite, so let's just say this one is at the top of the list. The panko-sesame crust keeps these pork cutlets crisp, but since they cook quickly, they remain juicy and super tender. And, of course, any excuse to serve a dish with mustard is a winner in my book. The spicier, the better. Speaking of mustard . . . Chinese mustard greens, known as *xuelihong*, can be found at your local Asian supermarket. If you can't find any (greens or markets, that is), you can easily swap them out with regular mustard greens or collard greens, removing and discarding the tough stems that run through the center of the leaves.

MAKES 4 SERVINGS

1 to 1½ pounds pork tenderloin, trimmed
Kosher salt and freshly ground black pepper
2 large eggs
1 cup panko bread crumbs
½ cup (about 2 ounces) white sesame seeds
½ cup high-heat oil, such as canola or safflower, divided
2 tablespoons sesame oil
4 medium cloves garlic, minced
2 teaspoons minced peeled fresh ginger

Pinch of red pepper flakes, or 1 small dried red chili pepper, seeded and chopped
1 pound Chinese mustard greens, chopped into 1-inch pieces
¼ cup chicken broth or water
3 tablespoons rice wine vinegar
1 tablespoon soy sauce
1 teaspoon white sugar
1 Asian pear, halved, cored, and thinly sliced or cut into 2-inch matchsticks
Spicy Chinese mustard, for serving

1   Preheat the oven to 200 degrees F.
2   Cut the tenderloin into eight equal pieces. Working with one piece at a time, place the pork between slices of parchment paper or plastic wrap and gently pound to ½ inch thick. Pat the pork dry with paper towels and season with salt and pepper.
3   Beat the eggs in a shallow dish with a little salt and pepper. Combine the panko and sesame seeds in a separate shallow bowl. Working with one piece at a time,

dip a cutlet in the egg mixture, allowing any extra to drip off, then coat in the sesame mixture, gently pressing to adhere. Transfer to a plate.

4   Heat ¼ cup of the high-heat oil in a 10-inch skillet over medium heat. Drop a small pinch of panko into the oil: when it turns golden brown, the oil is ready for cooking. Cook half the cutlets, without moving, until the bottoms are a deep golden brown, 2 to 3 minutes. Using tongs, carefully flip the cutlets and cook on the second side until a deep golden brown, 2 to 3 minutes more. Transfer the cutlets to a paper-towel-lined baking sheet and keep warm in the oven. Drain the oil from your skillet and wipe it clean. Add the remaining ¼ cup high-heat oil to the skillet and continue cooking the second half of the cutlets. Transfer the cutlets to the oven and wipe the skillet clean when finished.

5   Heat the sesame oil over medium heat. Add the garlic, ginger, and red pepper flakes and cook for 1 minute. Working in batches, stir in the mustard greens until wilted, 2 to 3 minutes. Add the broth, vinegar, soy sauce, and sugar and bring to a simmer. Cover with a lid, reduce the heat to low, and cook until the greens have softened, stirring often, 10 to 12 minutes. Remove the skillet from the heat and fold in the pears. Serve the pork over the greens with mustard on the side.

TIP: Coating the pork in the egg and sesame mixtures can be a messy business. To keep things *somewhat* cleaner, have a dedicated "egg hand" and a dedicated "panko hand;" otherwise you'll end up as coated as your cutlets.

HARISSA PORK CHOPS

with Eggplant, White Beans, and Tomatoes

If you don't have harissa on hand, you can either go get some (you can find it at most supermarkets or order it online), or you can make your own version for this recipe. Finely chop a few fresh red chilies and blend them with garlic, cumin seeds, and olive oil until smooth. I've kept this dish on the mild side so the eggplant and beans stand out without getting burned out. But if you like it spicy (like I do), serve extra harissa on the side.

MAKES 4 SERVINGS

4 (1-inch-thick) boneless pork chops, trimmed

Kosher salt and freshly ground black pepper

1 tablespoon high-heat oil, such as canola or safflower

1 tablespoon harissa sauce, plus more for schmearing

2 tablespoons unsalted butter

1 small yellow onion, chopped

1 medium eggplant (about ½ pound), cut into 1-inch cubes

4 medium cloves garlic, minced

1 (15-ounce) can fire-roasted diced tomatoes

1 (15-ounce) can cannellini or great northern beans, rinsed and drained

1 cup chicken broth or water

2 tablespoons chopped fresh mint

1 Season the pork chops with salt and pepper.

2 Heat the oil in a 10-inch skillet over medium heat. Add the pork chops and cook until browned, 2 to 3 minutes per side. Transfer to a plate and schmear with a touch of the harissa.

3 Melt the butter in your skillet over medium heat. Add the onions and cook until soft, about 5 minutes. Stir in the eggplant and cook until it begins to soften, about 5 minutes. Stir in the garlic and harissa and cook until fragrant, about 1 minute.

4 Add the tomatoes, beans, and broth to your skillet and bring to a boil. Nestle the pork chops in the sauce and reduce the heat to a simmer. Cover and cook until the pork reaches an internal temperature of 145 degrees F or the flesh is firm to the touch when prodded with a finger, 7 to 8 minutes. Garnish with the chopped mint before serving.

TIP: When choosing the perfect eggplant, look for one with smooth, shiny skin, a nice heft for its size, and firm flesh that gives a little when pressed with your thumb. In general, the smaller the eggplant, the sweeter the flesh and the more delicate the skin. You can use any variety of eggplant (from the common purple "globe" to the pretty and sweet "fairy tale" to the long and thin Japanese eggplant).

WINTER SQUASH COUSCOUS

with Pancetta

It's a combination of sweet (winter squash) and salty (pancetta), chewy (couscous) and crunchy (pepitas), all mixed together in one skillet. I suggest going light on the salt until the end of cooking—depending on your pancetta and pumpkin seeds, the sodium level can quickly add up. If you can't find winter squash (or are too busy to prepare your own), you can simply dump in a bag of diced frozen and defrosted squash when you bring the broth to a boil. Make sure to grab Israeli (pearl) couscous for this recipe, not the quick-cooking Moroccan couscous.

MAKES 4 SERVINGS

4 ounces pancetta, chopped into ¼-inch cubes
2 tablespoons extra-virgin olive oil
2 medium shallots, thinly sliced
1 pound winter squash (butternut, acorn, or pumpkin), peeled, seeded, and cut into ¾-inch pieces
3 medium cloves garlic, minced
1 teaspoon ground cumin
½ teaspoon smoked paprika

Pinch of red pepper flakes
1½ cups chicken broth
1 cup Israeli (pearl) couscous
¼ cup toasted pumpkin seeds (pepitas)
2 tablespoons freshly squeezed lemon juice
2 teaspoons fresh lemon zest
5 ounces baby spinach
Kosher salt and freshly ground black pepper

1   Heat a 10-inch skillet over medium heat. Add the pancetta and cook, stirring occasionally, until crisp and the fat is rendered, 5 to 7 minutes. Use a slotted spoon to transfer the pancetta to a plate; set aside.

2   Add the oil to the skillet with the pancetta fat. Cook the shallots until tender, about 5 minutes. Add the winter squash and cook, stirring frequently, until it begins to brown and soften, 6 to 8 minutes. Add the garlic, cumin, paprika, and red pepper flakes and cook until fragrant, about 1 minute.

3   Pour in the broth and bring to a boil. Stir in the couscous, cover, and reduce to a simmer. Cook until the couscous and squash are tender and most of the liquid is absorbed, 8 to 12 minutes.

4   Reduce the heat to low and fold in the reserved pancetta, pumpkin seeds, lemon juice, and lemon zest. Stir in the spinach, a handful at a time, until wilted, 3 to 5 minutes. Remove from the heat and season to taste with salt and pepper. Serve immediately.

SWAP IT OUT: Can't find pancetta? Swap it out with bacon, or crisp some prosciutto in your skillet for just a minute or two, then fold it into the finished dish along with the spinach.

SKILLET MAQUE CHOUX

with Andouille Sausage

Traditionally, *maque choux* (pronounced "mock shoe"), a corn-based Creole creation hailing from Louisiana, is served as a side dish. I upped the ante a bit, throwing in some spicy-but-not-too-hot andouille sausage and cayenne pepper, then mellowed the whole thing out with a bit of heavy cream. Yes, I love the flavor combination of the dish. But you know what I really love? I usually have most of the ingredients on hand (either in my freezer or fridge), and I can turn this into one of the world's quickest and easiest weeknight meals without a thought. Easy and delicious? *Laissez les bons temps rouler!**

*Let the good times roll!

MAKES 4 SERVINGS

1 tablespoon unsalted butter
8 ounces cured andouille sausage, diced
1 medium red bell pepper, chopped
1 small yellow onion, chopped
2 cups frozen corn, thawed
2 cups frozen sliced okra, thawed
3 medium cloves garlic, minced

1 tablespoon chopped fresh oregano, or 1 teaspoon dried
Pinch of cayenne pepper (optional)
Kosher salt and freshly ground black pepper
1 cup heavy cream or half-and-half
Cornbread, for serving (optional)

1   Melt the butter in a 10-inch skillet over medium heat. Add the sausage and cook, stirring occasionally, until lightly browned, 3 to 5 minutes. Add the peppers and onions and cook until soft, about 5 minutes. Stir in the corn and okra and cook until warmed through, 3 to 5 minutes more. Add the garlic, oregano, and cayenne pepper and cook until fragrant, about 1 minute. Season to taste with salt and pepper.

2   Pour in the cream and bring to a boil. Reduce the heat to a simmer and cook, stirring occasionally, until slightly thickened, 5 to 6 minutes. Divide between four bowls and serve with the cornbread.

ROASTED BRATWURST

with Apples, Radicchio, and White Beans

Sometimes life is a bit sweet, sometimes a little bitter, and if you put in some work at the beginning, with time and patience, there is usually a reward at the end. Whoa, I also just described this dinner! Sweet apples, bitter radicchio, and creamy beans are tossed with a sweet and pungent honey-mustard sauce that is the perfect balancing point for the dish. Juicy bratwurst are placed on top and the whole kit and kaboodle is popped into the oven. There's about five minutes of actual prep work that goes into this dish, forty-five minutes of doing whatever the heck you like with your time while dinner roasts, and a big payoff at the end with a complete and satisfying meal.

MAKES 4 SERVINGS

2 tablespoons extra-virgin olive oil

2 tablespoons stone-ground or whole-grain mustard, plus more for serving

1 tablespoon red wine vinegar

1 tablespoon honey

2 medium cloves garlic, minced

2 large sweet-tart apples, such as Gala or Honeycrisp, halved, cored, and thickly sliced

1 large head radicchio (about 8 ounces), cored and thickly sliced

1 small red onion, thickly sliced

Kosher salt and freshly ground black pepper

4 bratwurst sausages

1 (15-ounce) can great northern or cannellini beans, rinsed and drained

2 tablespoons chopped fresh parsley

1 Preheat the oven to 425 degrees F.
2 In a small bowl, whisk together the oil, mustard, vinegar, honey, and garlic.
3 In a 10-inch skillet, toss together the apples, radicchio, onions, and most of the vinaigrette. Season to taste with salt and pepper.
4 Pierce the bratwurst a few times with a fork. Add the bratwurst to the skillet and drizzle with the remaining vinaigrette.
5 Roast in the oven until the sausages and vegetables are browned and cooked through, about 40 minutes, flipping the bratwurst once halfway through cooking. Stir in the beans and continue to cook until warmed through, about 5 minutes more.
6 Carefully remove the skillet from the oven and sprinkle with the parsley. Serve with additional mustard.

TIP: No need to peel the apples; just core, slice, and go.

ACKNOWLEDGMENTS

Third time's a charm! Much like for the first two books, I would be remiss (and quite frankly, lost) without giving some of you special folks a shout-out for all of your hard work, support, guidance, and patience.

Partner in crime and husband extraordinaire, Evans Nguyen. I'm not sure who was more excited about this book—me, with my unending love for cast iron, or you, with your pure joy at getting to eat a meal, almost every night for months on end, laden with pork, beef, poultry, or fish. And yes, you nicely tolerated the vegetarian dishes too. Jack, Cole, and Ava, you willingly tried more dishes than I ever thought you would, ate considerable portions of them, and every once in a while snuck a second serving from our plates. If that's not a screaming round of approval, then I have no idea what is. Mom and Dad, you showed up to dinner more times than not and provided amazing child entertainment (and distraction) while I tested and retested recipes, in exchange for a family meal and leftovers to go home. It's funny how the tables have turned!

Where would I be without my amazing team of volunteer recipe testers? Some of you bravely came back from testing my first and second cookbooks, then incredibly asked for even more recipes to test than you were assigned. New testers popped out from the depths of social media and took a chance on a girl, a skillet, and a dream. Your feedback, comments, photos, and stories were invaluable in making these recipes perfect.

Last, but certainly not least, the amazing team at Sasquatch Books. You're like the perfect cast iron skillet: solid, trustworthy, well oiled (with a beautiful patina), and flexible to any need. The world's most fun editor to work with, Susan Roxborough, not only did you provide guidance for the book, you even volunteered to test recipes! And as Susan moved on to new adventures, publisher Jennifer Worick graciously stepped into her shoes with finesse and humor. A special shout out to all of those behind the scenes who make our books real and worthy: production and copy editors Bridget Sweet and Erin Cusick, photographer and food stylist for the interior Charity Burggraaf, and food stylist for the cover Jean Galton.

INDEX

Note: Page numbers in *italic* refer to photographs.

B

bacon
    Bacon and Poblano Grilled Cheese, 168, *169*
    Cheeseburger Macaroni, 135
    Clam and Bacon Pizza with Roasted Peppers,
        Kale, and Parmesan, *78*, 79–80
    Roasted Chicken with Braised White Beans and
        Bacon, 110, *111*
    Super-Fancy Bacon and Porcini Skillet Nachos,
        180, 181
beans
    Black Bean Chilaquiles with Eggs, *48*, 49
    Edamame-Ginger Rice with Chicken, *96*, 97
    Harissa Chickpeas with Eggs and Chard, 44
    Harissa Pork Chops with Eggplant, White Beans,
        and Tomatoes, 185
    Pan-Seared Gnocchi with Spinach and White
        Beans, *28*, 29
    Pasta e Ceci (Italian Pasta and Chickpea Stew),
        32, 33
    Roasted Bratwurst with Apples, Radicchio, and
        White Beans, *190*, 191
    Roasted Chicken with Braised White Beans and
        Bacon, 110, *111*
    Skirt Steak Street Tacos with Corn and Black
        Bean Salad, *140*, 141–142
    Spiced Beef and Chickpea–Stuffed Pitas
        "Kawarma," *154*, 155
    Three-Bean Tamale Pie, 45–46, *47*
beef, 125–157
    Beef, Green Bean, and Pineapple Red Curry,
        146, 147
    Cheeseburger Macaroni, 135
    Classic Patty Melts with Caramelized Onions and
        Cheddar, 143
    Good Ol' Beef Pot Pie, *148*, 149–150
    Herb-Crusted Flank Steak with Sauteed Grapes
        and Blue Cheese, *138*, 139
    Meatballs with Caramelized Onions and Pine Nut
        Lemon Rice, 130, *131*
    Pan-Seared New York Steak with Tarragon
        Mustard and Spring Vegetables, *144*, 145
    Reuben Dutch Baby, 136, *137*
    Root Vegetable and Beef Skillet Gratin, 151–152,
        153
    Seared Rib-Eye Steak with Wilted Napa Cabbage,
        156, 157
    Skillet Inside-Out Taco Bake, 129

    Skirt Steak Street Tacos with Corn and Black
        Bean Salad, *140*, 141–142
    Spiced Beef and Chickpea–Stuffed Pitas
        "Kawarma," *154*, 155
    Steak Tips and Cauliflower "Caponata" Salad,
        132, 133–134
    Stir-Fried Teriyaki Beef with Broccoli, *126*, 127–128
Biscuits, Cheddar Buttermilk, *100*, 101–102

C

cast iron, tips and tricks for using, 4–15
Cauliflower and Eggplant Masala, *36*, 37
Cauliflower "Caponata" Salad, Steak Tips and, *132*,
    133–134
Chard, Harissa Chickpeas with Eggs and, 44
Cheeseburger Macaroni, 135
chicken. *See* poultry
Chilaquiles with Eggs, Black Bean, *48*, 49
Chili with Cheddar Buttermilk Biscuits, Turkey
    Skillet, *100*, 101–102
clams. *See* seafood
Cornish Game Hens with Roasted Beets and
    Pistachios, Orange-Tarragon, 114, *115*
Couscous, Chicken Thighs with Broccolini, Lemon,
    and Israeli, 119–120, *121*
Couscous Salad, Curry Poached Chicken and,
    91–92, *93*
Couscous with Pancetta, Winter Squash, 186, *187*
curry
    Beef, Green Bean, and Pineapple Red Curry,
        146, 147
    Curry Poached Chicken and Couscous Salad,
        91–92, *93*
    Thai Green Curry with Tofu and Rice Cakes, *38*,
        39–40
    Thai Red Curry Rice with Halibut, *62*, 63

D

Duck Breasts with Fig and Arugula Salad, Seared,
    112, 113
Dutch Baby, Reuben, 136, *137*

E

Eggplant Masala, Cauliflower and, *36*, 37
Enchilada Skillet, Easy Chicken, 109

F

fish
Baked Cod with Artichokes, Sun-Dried Tomatoes, and Olives, 52, *53*
Brown Butter Halibut with Celeriac, 56, *57*
Glazed Salmon with Black-Eyed Peas, Pomegranate Seeds, and Arugula, 69–70, *71*
Pan-Seared Salmon with Braised Lentil Salad, *54*, 55
Smoked Salmon Frittata with Cream Cheese, Capers, and Dill, 81
Thai Red Curry Rice with Halibut, *62, 63*
Tomato-Poached Mahi with Zucchini and Fresh Herbs, *84*, 85
Tuna Noodle Skillet Casserole with Peas and Prosciutto, 82, *83*
Frittata with Cream Cheese, Capers, and Dill, Smoked Salmon, 81
Frittata with Piquillo Peppers and Artichokes, Pasta, 24

G

Gnocchi with Spinach and White Beans, Pan-Seared, *28, 29*
Gratin, Root Vegetable and Beef Skillet, 151–152, *153*
Grilled Cheese, Bacon and Poblano, 168, *169*

H

Hash with Italian Sausage, Yam and Beet, 178, *179*

M

Maque Choux with Andouille Sausage, Skillet, *188,* 189
Masala, Cauliflower and Eggplant, *36, 37*
Meatballs with Caramelized Onions and Pine Nut Lemon Rice, 130, *131*
mussels. *See* seafood

N

Nachos, Super-Fancy Bacon and Porcini Skillet, *180,* 181
noodles. *See* pasta

O

Onion and Tomato Pie, Caramelized, 25–26, *27*
Onion Soup-Strata, French, 41
Orzotto with Fennel, Orange, and Goat Cheese, Scallop, 64, *65*

P

Paella with Mussels and Chorizo, Weeknight Orzo, 66, *67–68*
pasta
Cheeseburger Macaroni, 135
Clam Fideos, 60, *61*
"Kids' Favorite, The" Skillet Lasagna, 163
Orecchiette with Butternut Squash, Leeks, and Sage, *18, 19–20*
Orzo with Asparagus, Peas, and Parmesan, 34, *35*
Pasta e Ceci (Italian Pasta and Chickpea Stew), *32,* 33
Pasta Frittata with Piquillo Peppers and Artichokes, 24
Pork Ramen with Bamboo and Mushrooms, *170,* 171–172
Skillet Mussel Marinara, *72,* 73
Stir-Fried Teriyaki Beef with Broccoli, *126,* 127–128
Tuna Noodle Skillet Casserole with Peas and Prosciutto, 82, *83*
Weeknight Orzo Paella with Mussels and Chorizo, 66, *67–68*
Patty Melts with Caramelized Onions and Cheddar, Classic, 143
Pisto Manchego (Spanish Ratatouille), 42, *43*
Pitas "Kawarma," Spiced Beef and Chickpea–Stuffed, *154,* 155
Pizza with Roasted Peppers, Kale, and Parmesan, Clam and Bacon, *78,* 79–80
pork, 159–191
See also bacon; sausage
Caraway-Crusted Pork Tenderloin with Sauerkraut and Apples, *176,* 177
Grits-Crusted Ham and Cheese Quiche, 164–165
Harissa Pork Chops with Eggplant, White Beans, and Tomatoes, 185
"Kids' Favorite, The" Skillet Lasagna, 163
Mustard-Coated Pork Tenderloin with Green Beans and Potatoes, *166,* 167
Pork Chops with Cashew-Lime Rice, *160,* 161–162
Pork Ramen with Bamboo and Mushrooms, *170,* 171–172
Sesame Pork Cutlets with Warm Mustard Greens, *182,* 183–184
Tuna Noodle Skillet Casserole with Peas and Prosciutto, 82, *83*
Winter Squash Couscous with Pancetta, 186, *187*
Pot Pie, Good Ol' Beef, *148,* 149–150
Pot Pie with a Twist, Turkey, *94,* 95
poultry, 87–123
Chicken Tagine with Spiced Fennel Quinoa, *106,* 107–108
Chicken Thighs with Broccolini, Lemon, and Israeli Couscous, 119–120, *121*
Curry Poached Chicken and Couscous Salad, 91–92, *93*

Dijon-Roasted Chicken with Italian Sausage and
    Brussels Sprouts, *122*, 123
Easy Chicken Enchilada Skillet, 109
Edamame-Ginger Rice with Chicken, 96, *97*
Glazed Chicken Drumsticks with Warm Carrot
    Salad, 103–104, *105*
Miso Chicken with Bok Choy and Mushrooms,
    88, 89–90
Orange-Tarragon Cornish Game Hens with
    Roasted Beets and Pistachios, 114, *115*
Parmesan Chicken Tenders with Warm Fennel,
    Apple, and Arugula Salad, *116*, 117–118
Roasted Chicken with Braised White Beans and
    Bacon, 110, *111*
Roasted Chicken with New Potatoes, Coriander,
    and Mint, 98, 99
Seared Duck Breasts with Fig and Arugula Salad,
    112, 113
Turkey Pot Pie with a Twist, 94, 95
Turkey Skillet Chili with Cheddar Buttermilk
    Biscuits, *100*, 101–102

Q

Quesadillas, Chorizo and Sweet Potato, 173–174, *175*
Quiche, Grits-Crusted Ham and Cheese, 164–165

R

Ratatouille, Spanish (Pisto Manchego), 42, *43*
Reuben Dutch Baby, 136, *137*
rice
    Edamame-Ginger Rice with Chicken, 96, *97*
    Ginger Shrimp and Sugar Snap Peas with
        Coconut Rice, 75–76, *77*
    Kimchi Fried Rice with Enoki Mushrooms and
        Tofu, 30, *31*
    Meatballs with Caramelized Onions and Pine Nut
        Lemon Rice, 130, *131*
    Pork Chops with Cashew-Lime Rice, *160*, 161–162
    Thai Green Curry with Tofu and Rice Cakes, 38,
        39–40
    Thai Red Curry Rice with Halibut, 62, 63

S

salads
    Black-Eyed Peas, Pomegranate Seeds, and
        Arugula, 69–70, *71*
    Braised Lentil Salad, *54*, 55
    Cauliflower "Caponata" Salad, *132*, 133–134
    Corn and Black Bean Salad, *140*, 141–142
    Curry Poached Chicken and Couscous Salad,
        91–92, *93*
    Fig and Arugula Salad, *112*, 113
    Warm Carrot Salad, 103–104, *105*

Warm Fennel, Apple, and Arugula Salad, *116*,
    117–118
sausage
    Chorizo and Sweet Potato Quesadillas, 173–174,
        175
    Dijon-Roasted Chicken with Italian Sausage and
        Brussels Sprouts, *122*, 123
    Roasted Bratwurst with Apples, Radicchio, and
        White Beans, 190, *191*
    Skillet Maque Choux with Andouille Sausage,
        188, 189
    Skillet Shrimp "Boil" with Potatoes, Corn, and
        Sausage, 58, 59
    Weeknight Orzo Paella with Mussels and Chorizo,
        66, 67–68
    Yam and Beet Hash with Italian Sausage, 178, *179*
seafood, 51–85
    See also fish
    Clam and Bacon Pizza with Roasted Peppers,
        Kale, and Parmesan, 78, 79–80
    Clam Fideos, 60, *61*
    Ginger Shrimp and Sugar Snap Peas with
        Coconut Rice, 75–76, *77*
    mussels, how to pick, 74
    Scallop Orzotto with Fennel, Orange, and Goat
        Cheese, 64, *65*
    Skillet Mussel Marinara, *72*, 73
    Skillet Shrimp "Boil" with Potatoes, Corn, and
        Sausage, *58*, 59
    Weeknight Orzo Paella with Mussels and Chorizo,
        66, 67–68
Soup-Strata, French Onion, 41
Spanakopita, Cheater's Skillet, 21–22, *23*
Squash, Leeks, and Sage, Orecchiette with
    Butternut, *18*, 19–20
Squash Couscous with Pancetta, Winter, 186, *187*
Stew, Italian Pasta and Chickpea, 32, *33*

T

Taco Bake, Skillet Inside-Out, 129
Tacos with Corn and Black Bean Salad, Skirt Steak
    Street, *140*, 141–142
Tagine with Spiced Fennel Quinoa, Chicken, *106*,
    107–108
Tamale Pie, Three-Bean, 45–46, *47*
Tomato Pie, Caramelized Onion and, 25–26, *27*
turkey. *See* poultry

V

vegetarian dishes, 17–49

Printed in China

SASQUATCH BOOKS with colophon is a registered trademark of Penguin Random House LLC

26 25 24 23 22   9 8 7 6 5 4 3 2 1

Editors: Susan Roxborough and Jen Worick
Production editor: Bridget Sweet
Designer: Tony Ong
Photographs: Charity Burggraaf
Cover food styling: Jean Galton
Interior food styling: Charity Burggraaf

Library of Congress Cataloging-in-Publication Data
Names: Freeman, Jackie, author.
Title: Cast iron skillet one-pan meals : 75 family-friendly recipes for
   everyday dinners / Jackie Freeman.
Description: Seattle : Sasquatch Books, [2022] | Includes index.
Identifiers: LCCN 2022003185 (print) | LCCN 2022003186 (ebook) | ISBN
   9781632174208 (paperback) | ISBN 9781632174215 (epub)
Subjects: LCSH: Skillet cooking. | Cast-iron. | One-dish meals. | Dinners
   and dining. | LCGFT: Cookbooks.
Classification: LCC TX840.S55 F75 2022 (print) | LCC TX840.S55 (ebook) |
   DDC 641.7/7--dc23/eng/20220211
LC record available at https://lccn.loc.gov/2022003185
LC ebook record available at https://lccn.loc.gov/2022003186

ISBN: 978-1-63217-420-8

Sasquatch Books
1325 Fourth Avenue, Suite 1025
Seattle, WA 98101
SasquatchBooks.com